CLASS 37s
AT WORK

CLASS 37s AT WORK

Michael J. Collins

LONDON
IAN ALLAN LTD

First published 1984

ISBN 0 7110 1447 7

© Ian Allan Ltd 1984

Published by Ian Allan Ltd, Shepperton, Surrey;
and printed by Ian Allan Printing Ltd at their works
at Coombelands in Runnymede, England.

To my wife and children,
without whose support and help
this book could never have
been written.

Contents

Cover:
No 37.290 joins the main line and descends towards the Severn Tunnel with a ballast train at Caldicot, on 27 March 1982.
Les Bertram

Previous page:
Full yellow ends, BR blue colour scheme and number without the 'D' prefix are sported by No 6724 as it rolls through the Suffolk countryside with a lengthy Whitemoor (March)-Ipswich freight on 7 September 1970,
G. R. Mortimer

Left:
A very crisp photograph of green-liveried English Electric Type 3 No D6720 heading up the East Coast main line with a very mixed freight during the early 1960s. The snow is reflecting enough light under the bogies to give detail on the complex pipe work situated under the buffers.

Introduction

Just over 300 of the English Electric Type 3s, later known as BR Class 37s, were built between the middle of 1960 and the beginning of January 1966. In 24 years the class has travelled many millions of miles in service; it has visited almost every corner of mainland Britain and hauled virtually every type of train which runs on the BR network. The origins of the locomotive, particularly its 12CSVT prime mover, can be traced back for nearly 40 years and the oldest machines are now approaching their quarter century in service — a remarkable achievement for any internal combustion-engined machine.

I can still remember, with some affection, my first introduction to the class when, as a schoolboy, I visited Norwich Thorpe station during the summer of 1961. Here I saw No D6707 at the head of an express to Liverpool Street.

The clean green lines of the locomotive made an immediate impression; its distinctive sound, its throaty roar when accelerating away with a train, the body-sides displaying a stylish 'tumble-home' at skirt level and the evocative nose so characteristic of English Electric products of the time, all added to that first immediate impression. The introduction of the class had spelt the end for 'Britannia' Pacific steam locomotives on Norwich line expresses, but to my mind here was a machine that was a worthy successor. What a pity that in performance the then new diesel never quite reached the level obtainable with the steam locomotives which it replaced.

In this book it has been my intention to produce a balanced account which incorporates a technical appreciation, a historical synopsis, a recognition guide, and an idea

Left:
The line to Botley Stone Terminal, Hampshire, follows the alignment of the former branch to Bishop's Waltham. Here, Nos 37.159 and 37.288 are framed by part of the station canopy as they back 'Foster Yeoman' hoppers from Westbury into the terminal on 3 December 1983. *Michael J. Collins*

Right:
An overnight air-braked freight from Duxford, Cambridgeshire, is caught taking a short pause at York station on 6 April 1983 with No 37.048 at the front. *Michael J. Collins*

of what Class 37s are really like at work on British Rail. Comprehensive appendices have been provided ranging from details of major components to a tabulated cab layout guide. Over 200 photographs are included to show the locomotives at work in all corners of Britain during a period spanning the service years of the class.

The aim of the book is not to refer to the class as something extraordinary, nor to enhance its reputation, nor to enter into any particular debate about its usefulness. It is merely to show the locomotives as they are — good solid workhorses, reliable to the extreme and the masters of almost any working on BR which runs within their 90mph capability. Equally at home slogging upgrade with an enormous load of freight or thrashing up the main line with a passenger train they are a classic mixed-traffic type. Above all they are an engineman's machine, being good natured maids of all work. Their at times 90% availability makes them a diagrammer's machine too. Glamorous, no, but the class still attracts a tremendous following by enthusiasts and railway staff alike. If my own personal liking for the machines comes through in the book I make no apology!

Fortunately the class is not scheduled for early withdrawal; indeed plans exist to keep it running at least until the year 2000 and probably beyond. Only one unit has suffered the ignominy of withdrawal and scrapping after being so badly damaged as a result of a collision that it was considered beyond economic repair.

Not many years ago it hardly seemed likely that a class of diesel locomotives, such as the Class 37s, would form the basis for a monologue which had commercial possibilities. The current surge of interest in English Electric products fostered by the demise of their sister machines, the Class 40s, coupled with the charisma attached to the Class 50s, has made this book possible.

The photographs in this book could not have been of such high quality or covered the geography of the British Isles so fully without the assistance of very many fellow railway photographers, and my thanks go to them all. Colin Marsden, Michael Hunt and Mike Woodhouse have given valuable assistance on technical matters. Michael Oakley made a significant contribution to the book when he kindly undertook to prepare the chapter on Class 37s in service. A mention must go to John Day, of the Ipswich Transport Society, who has been a tower of strength, accompanying me on many long photographic forays in researching Class 37 workings. Finally, a tribute should go to my publishers, who have allowed me complete freedom to develop this book as I wish. Many hours have been spent both at the typewriter and at the lineside in preparing it, and I hope that readers derive much enjoyment from browsing through this volume in the series.

Michael J. Collins
Colchester

1
The Origins and Concept of the Design

When British Railways was formed in 1948, steam traction still reigned supreme because a fleet of several thousand steam locomotives covered virtually all haulage requirements. The only diesel working was confined to a small number of ex-LMS shunters and a few ex-GWR diesel railcars. Indeed, at this time a number of steam-powered BR Standard designs were being put forward for consideration under the direction of Mr R. A. Riddles. For seven years this comfortable state of affairs continued with only a small number of additional diesel shunters appearing, and seeming to offer little or no threat to the supremacy of steam traction.

The publication, in 1955, of the British Railways Modernisation Plan, under the auspices of the British Transport Commission, in many ways shook to the roots current thinking by the railway authorities and railway enthusiasts alike. The plan envisaged the demise of steam propulsion and its replacement using traction units utilising either internal combustion engines or electric power. It was the speed of replacement which was particularly surprising because the Modernisation Plan saw a time scale of only 20 years until final replacement of steam traction. It was thought that the use of the alternative forms of power was the key to obtaining a better thermal efficiency and a far better service reliability and availability from traction units.

The Modernisation Plan came along before any hint of world oil shortages and spiralling costs of petro-chemical based products; the BTC wanted to move towards what it saw as gains in efficiency with some dispatch. In order to instigate some movement in this direction and to encourage thinking towards the use of diesel power for rail traction a 'Pilot Scheme' was authorised as part of the Modernisation Plan. Under the wording of the Pilot Scheme, diesel manufacturers could build prototypes at their own expense using their own resources. The resulting machines could then be submitted to BR for rigorous testing and evaluation under both service conditions and laboratory environments with a possibility of further orders by BR if the machines proved satisfactory. It was in response to this invitation that the English Electric Co designed and built its 2,000 brake horsepower (bhp) 1Co-Co1 design (later known as the Class 40) which is directly related to the Class 37 derivative.

At this point it would clarify the picture if mention was made to the state of affairs appertaining to diesel locomotives and their development in the years prior to 1948. After the financial rigours and stringencies of World War 2, when investment resources, skilled manpower and climate for change had been at a low ebb, the railways of Britain were in a very depressed state. Money was being diverted from investment in order to merely keep going. But at this time, after the damage by enemy action and the cessation of hostilities, talk was of reconstruction. Rumours emanated from the Head Offices of all the 'big four' railway companies about possible alternatives to steam power.

Experience in diesel traction had, up to that time, been quite limited. The LMR had run a small fleet of diesel shunters but few other significant diesel-powered machines were running on the railways of Britain. It was in the USA that skill and expertise in the running of a diesel fleet was available. Therefore a party of Southern Railway officials crossed the Atlantic to study the problems and possible benefits which could be gained from developing diesel traction. They must have been impressed because, in late autumn 1946, the Southern Railway took the initiative and publicised its intention to build three 1,600bhp diesels, and to put them into service on the ex-LSWR main line from Waterloo to Exeter and beyond. The project did suffer from prolonged delays, however, and the first locomotive did not come out of the workshop for public scrutiny until 1950.

Quite independently, the LMS also devised plans to enter into the arena of high-horsepower diesel-powered locomotion. An invitation went out to the English Electric Co to collaborate with the LMS in the production of two diesel-electric locomotives with a designed bhp of 1,600 each. The idea was for English Electric to provide primary power units and transmission equipment for the project, leaving the LMS engineers to organise other items such as superstructure and bogies. These LMS locomotives must be discussed in some detail because they had a significant influence on later designs coming from the English Electric Co, including the Class 40s and their cousins the Class 37s.

On 5 December 1947 the first of the two machines, numbered 10000, proudly emerged from No 10A shop at Derby Works. Finished in black, with a prominent white line encircling the locomotive at waist level, the machine had the conspicuous nose ends associated with American practice of the time. These embellishments were an attempt to solve the constraints imposed by the British loading gauge, where space was at a premium. The nose ends were a convenient place to house such essential auxiliary equipment as traction motor blowers and air compressors. In addition it was thought that they offered drivers some measure of protection in the sad event of a collision. Also it was thought prudent to restrict the driver's view of the track immediately in front of the locomotive. This was because some academics and scholars of the time were worried about possible hypnotic effects which might ensue if personnel had an uninterrupted view of the track and associated sleeper work at high speed. The noses, therefore, were an important aspect of English Electric Co design and remained so when the Class 37s were constructed some 13 years later.

The diesel engine used to power No 10000 was the same English Electric vee-form 16-cylinder power unit which has been developed by the company to its ultimate in today's traction units. In No 10000 it was set a continuous rating of 1,600bhp at 750rpm. The engine was known, in English Electric parlance, as the 16CSVT (16-cylinder, supercharged, vee-form, rail traction engine). The Southern Region authorities were impressed by its characteristics, as used in both 10000 and 10001, and decided to use the engine in the three machines of Southern Railway origin mentioned earlier — by this time nationalisation had taken place and the Southern Region of British Railways had inherited the construction of these three machines because they had not been completed prior to nationalisation. Essentially the same power unit was incorporated into the Class 40 design and a derivative power unit went into the Class 37s.

The chassis and frame of the two LMS locomotives were fashioned from long steel joists made from girders of 'I' cross section. Cross members added strength and rigidity to these frames and formed supports for deck plates to be added, upon which were mounted the power units and auxiliary equipment. The 'strength underframe' technique of construction, with body and superstructure taking no load, was employed on all subsequent English Electric locomotives built for British Railways including, of course, the three locomotives for the Southern Region and ultimately the Class 37s.

Although the product was publicised a year before the LMS project, the Southern diesels did not see the light of day until November 1950. These machines had taken four years to design and construct, in stark contrast to the seven months required to produce No 10000. The very first of the Southern diesels was numbered 10201, and the second machine, numbered 10202, emerged from Ashford Works in August 1950. They were a joint design by English Electric and O. V. S. Bulleid, Chief Mechanical and Electrical Engineer of the Southern Railway. The 1Co-Co1 wheel arrangement differed from the Co-Co of the LMS products and the new machines lacked the prominent nose ends of the Derby locomotive. Externally the body-sides of the SR product displayed the gently rounded cross section whcih was reminiscent of the profile of the Southern rolling stock which was in use at that time. The 16CSVT engine was a common feature of both designs and the internal workings of both machines were very similar.

The Co-Cos, Nos 10000 and 10001, had all of the axles on each bogie powered by axle-hung nose-suspended traction motors. Originally their weight in working order was 127ton 13cwt but later modifications to the train heating arrangements increased their weights by three tons. The civil

engineering authorities had been satisfied with their axle loadings and they had been passed for main line running. From the inception of the dieselisation experiment, the civil engineers had voiced caution over the likely effects on their track of the small diameter powered wheels of diesel-electrics. This was because they carried a great deal more weight per inch of their tread in relation to that carried by those of steam locomotives. They pointed to horror stories emanating from the United States, but these were not really justified because most of the track damage cited by American engineers was blamed on wheelslip under massive braking loads which home-produced diesels would never have to cope with. Caution prevailed, however, and the Southern machines had huge plate frame bogies fitted in an attempt to spread the load. These in themselves gave extra weight and the SR machines were some eight tons heavier than their LMR counterparts. Problems for these machines were compounded because the British civil engineers were uncertain of the effect that diesel technology would have on bridge work and other engineering edifices so the Southern authorities preferred to err on the safe side. So, from the very beginning, Nos 10201 and 10202 were stricken with chronic weight and axle load disadvantages because the 1Co-Co1 wheel arrangement was forced upon them.

The increase in weight of the SR machines made it desirable for more power to be developed by the traction unit and it was perhaps fortunate that the 16CSVT had been improved to 1,750bhp by the time of their introduction. Extra power could be developed because an improvement in the turbocharging system was found to be possible by replacing the Brown-Boveri blowers of Nos 10000 and 10001 by units manufactured by D. Napier & Son — an English Electric subsidiary company. This product has been used in conjunction with the English Electric vee range of engines from this time onwards and has, indeed, been incorporated into the engine fitted into the Class 37s.

Experience gained in service was applied to the third Southern diesel, No 10203, which was released from Brighton Works in early March 1954. It was externally similar to the two original machines, but sported the 16CSVT engine in its Mk II form, allowing extra power to be developed. It was also lighter at 132 ton 16cwt, and design improvements allowed the pneumatic control system to provide stepless variation of engine speed through the whole range of engine speed from 450rpm to 850rpm. This resulted in a marked improvement in handling, the old notch system acting in such a way that it hampered the selection of engine speeds coinciding with the crankshaft critical speeds.

Therefore No 10203 was a considerable improvement on all four of the earlier machines referred to above. This was manifested later when, after transfer to the LMR, it was regularly rostered to haul the 'Royal Scot' single-handed. Operating authorities preferred to use the other machines on this duty in pairs. The fact remains, however, that the entire batch of Southern diesels were elephantine beasts — cumbersome, overweight, lumbering machines, restricted in the routes that they could use and always suffering from an extremely poor power-to-weight ratio. It is ironic that the same criticism could be levelled at most of the later 'Pilot Scheme' diesels, and in particular to those that became known as Classes 40, 44, 45 and 46. All of these machines consumed far too much of their own engine output by simply overcoming the inertia developed by their own enormous bulk. All were severely hampered by the same 1Co-Co1 wheel arrangement. The heavy V16 engine, without charge-air after cooling and of only 2,000bhp output at the time of order, simply did not develop enough power to counteract this enormous bulk.

The operating authorities eventually became very disillusioned by the early diesels which were consequently the subject of much criticism from railway operatives and management. In hindsight, some consideration must be given to other factors influencing the performance of these locomotives. Their great weight was to some measure attributable to the construction of the machines using steam age skills, materials and technology. Modern alloys were simply not available. In any case the 'Pilot Scheme' diesels were very much innovative products from which a great deal was learned and applied in later building projects. At this time, servicing facilities were basic in the extreme. Most mainten-ance was carried out amongst the filth and grime of a steam locomotive shed. Such muck and dust is an anathema to any internal combustion machine and the early diesels were no exception. Personnel were largely inexperienced and only trained in the basic principles of the intricacies of the diesel engine and its associated auxiliaries. This was the lot of the early diesels, but without their design and parentage the Class 37s would not have been built.

After ordering a fleet of nearly 400 of these large 1Co-Co1 machines and gaining considerable servicing and operating experience with them, British Railways realised that what they really required was a versatile mixed traffic diesel unit without such heavy construction. This would allow a light axle loading and a high power-to-weight ratio machine to be constructed. The Class 37 was designed to fill this niche admirably.

WR Passenger Workings

Top left:
Snowplough-fitted No 37.175 makes an unusual sight at the Paddington buffer stops after arriving with the 08.08 service from Hereford, on 14 January 1980. Consideration was given in the mid-1970s for the use of Class 37s regularly on the Hereford line service but this did not come to fruition.
Bert Wynn

Bottom left:
Complete with Central Wales line headlamp fitted by means of a bar secured to special nose brackets, No 37.182 arrives at Newport with ECS on 11 September 1978. The stock will form the 17.05 service to Swansea. Recently, BR has decreed that all locomotives capable of working at over 90mph should be headlight fitted, but how they will be permanently attached to Class 37s remains to be seen. *Geoff Dowling*

Right, top to bottom:
Passenger services in West Wales were Class 37-hauled for a couple of years in the early 1980s but such trains are now handled by Class 33s working on long cyclic diagrams from Eastleigh. Passing Tenby box is No 37.186 while hauling the four-coach 19.00 service to Swansea on 19 August 1981. *Michael J. Collins*

Only a few passengers wait for the 16.10 Swansea-Pembroke Dock stopping train on 18 August 1981. The formation is pictured entering Whitland station on a sunny evening. *Michael J. Collins*

Heading west, No 37.190 passes near to Llanllwch, Carmarthen while hauling the 11.15 Swansea-Milford Haven stopping service on 18 August 1981. *Michael J. Collins*

2
Power Unit: History and Development

It may come as a surprise to learn that the English Electric Co, formed in 1918, has foundations in the construction of engines dating back to the Beardmore power units used to propel Britain's biggest airship, the R101. This was constructed in 1924 but following a disastrous crash in 1930 near Beauvais, France interest in airships gradually waned. The development programme for the airships was subsequently abandoned.

The possibility of redundancy and unemployment encouraged some of the Beardmore design staff to join the English Electric Co. The Beardmore diesel had by then become sophisticated and highly developed and in it can be found the beginnings of the English Electric K type engine introduced in 1934. This engine was installed in the LMS diesel shunters and later in the familiar and ubiquitous British Railways Class 08 shunter. A development of the K type engine was the RK version, with vee-form variants, having the same 10in (254mm) cylinder base and 12in (305mm) piston stroke of the original engine. This was considered to be more suitable for main line diesel locomotion.

It is this vee series engine which is relevant to this chapter because a derivative of the design forms the prime mover of the Class 37. Development and research was on-going, but versions came in logical steps. The important features of each variant to see service on British Railways are outlined, so that the development of the English Electric power unit used in the Class 37 can be seen within its historical setting.

All of the versions of the vee-type engine, including the 12CSVT power unit of the Class 37, are medium speed, four stroke, single-acting engines with direct injection. They have a 45° angle between each bank of cylinders.

The first vee-type engine developed by English Electric was the 16CSVT Mk I (the engine referred to in Chapter 1) and fitted to Nos 10000 and 10001. It was a 16-cylinder supercharged vee-form engine rated at 1600bhp at 750rpm. This meant that each cylinder developed 100bhp. The basic engine weight was 38,550lb and mathematics tells us that 24.1lb were needed for each developed horsepower. Peak pressure was given as 900lb/sq in and the Brake Mean Effective Pressure (BMEP) was quoted as 99lb/sq in. Incorporated within the design were two-valve cylinder heads, white metal main and big end bearings, and a British Brown-Boveri turbo-charger set. A number of elements within the design

were inherited from the K range, in particular bevel gear drives for the water and oil pumps, camshafts using a chain drive, and a crankcase without the refinement of being dynamically balanced. The latter was a retrograde step and was incorporated as a cost cutting exercise. Control was 'notched' rather than continuously variable and gave three engine speeds in conjunction with three differing degrees of generator excitation.

The 16CSVT (Mk II), used on Southern Railway Nos 10201 and 10202 of 1950, was rated at some 10% over the preceding engine, delivering a nominal 1,760bhp at 750rpm. Unfortunately notched control was used again but developments within this Mark were copper-lead main and big end bearings, CAV fuel injection, and the Napier TS100 turbochargers.

Diesel engine technology was still rapidly developing and many lessons were learned at this time from both engines. Failures attributable to engine breakdown and malfunction were common because both variants of the machine suffered from turbo-charger surging and seizures. Another problem arose because the chamshaft chains were without an automatic tensioning device and therefore needed frequent adjustment to ensure maximum efficiency. Generators failed quite frequently because crankcase pressure would often force oil right through the crankcase labyrinth seals and into the generator assembly, thus preventing an adequate electrical output. Problems were experienced with joints which had to be fashioned on to the exhaust pipes and they frequently allowed hot exhaust gases to leak and start a conflagration or smouldering fire in the lagging. Learning and consequent development from the experience gained took place as a function of an increasing awareness of the problems which could be thrown up by these motors when in service. As a result of this experience further development took place and in March 1954 the 16 CSVT Mk II was installed in the third of the 'Southern' diesels, No 10203.

The new model delivered 2,000bhp at 850rpm for an engine weight of 40,760lb, giving 20.41lb/hp, an advantage of 3.71lb/hp over the original 16CSVT engines fitted to Nos 10000 and 10001. Piston speed was 1,700 strokes per minute with peak pressure being 950lb/sq in and BMEP at 124lb/sq in. The design utilised a number of radical improvements but perhaps the most important was that at last a pneumatic speed control was fitted. The device allowed continuous torque regulation over the range 480 to 850rpm — from idling speed to full power. The propensity of the previous engines to catch alight was countered by the fitting of bellows joints in the exhaust manifolds. The problems arising through engine oil finding its way into the generator set was solved by fitting the crankcase breather so that it vented into the radiator fan chamber. Other improvements included new four-valve cylinder heads, thin wall copper-lead big end bearings and a pressure-fed fuel system. In addition the larger Napier MS100 (formerly designated TS100/4) turbochargers were fitted. In contrast, however, it was surprising that some inherent weaknesses of the design remained unaltered in the new version. The unbalanced crankshaft, referred to earlier, was retained as were the camshaft driving chains — considered very crude by today's standards. Restraints caused by the British loading gauge made it necessary for four turbo-chargers to be utilised since two of the size deemed necessary could not be accommodated within the loading gauge.

This engine was selected for use in the D200-D209 (English Electric Type 4, BR Class 40) locomotives then being constructed under the Pilot Scheme invitation. These were ordered on 16 November 1955. The engine was chosen without any modifications because it was considered vital to get the machines 'on the road' without undue delay so that they could prove themselves and perhaps attract further orders. Indeed, the engine was employed in all the D200 build, with the refinement of an improved 'inclined bolt' big end incorporated. This innovation was first tried on No 10203, and permitted connecting rods to be withdrawn in situ with their attached piston as one unit instead of being withdrawn divorced from each other, as previously required in earlier engines necessitating removal through the crankcase doors.

At this point a change in company policy had its effect. Having developed the 16CSVT Mk II as a reliable and stalwart performer, the company embarked on a programme designed to develop a traction oil engine aimed at meeting a variety of applications. Funding and skilled engineers, therefore, were diverted away from the RK vee range. In retrospect this can be seen as a misguided decision because it was at this time that development of the RK range was most needed. The thinking behind the decision was that English Electric had a history of being vigilant in its search for lucrative export opportunities and the oil engine project was seen to have such potential. In addition, at this time BR management was cool towards the idea of using a higher performance diesel prime mover in its traction units. This was because BR was still influenced by performance obtained with steam traction. It held the opinion that the 2,000bhp obtained with present machinery would be more than adequate for the performance required at the time and for the immediate future; it prevailed with the view that this would produce a traction unit easily equivalent to the best steam locomotives available for traffic.

Another factor working against English Electric at this time was that investment for new designs was allocated to a not too successful range of quick-running engines. Work on this programme started during March 1958 at an allocated cost of £850,000. The new engines were thought to be the answer for competition from American and continental competitors for sales in developing nations. Research engineers were briefed to succeed in producing a 1,500rpm lightweight

Below:
A fine view of No 37.080 crossing high above the River Tyne with a long rake of parcels and newspaper stock. Note the two coaches from a Metro-Cammell three-car DMU marshalled next to the engine. *John Whitehouse*

engine for application in narrow gauge locomotives. For five years, investment was ploughed into several projects, four of which never proceeded beyond the prototype stage. The whole scheme was abandoned in 1963, having eaten up £1.2million of English Electric research and development funds.

By 1960 English Electric's big competitor, Sulzer Brothers, was in a position to offer its 12LDA28 at 2,750bhp — a 10% uprating. It became clear that English Electric was rapidly falling behind in the development of higher powers. One of the factors operating against the company was its method of engine price calculation. Shortly after the company's formation, each of its four main constituent works at Stafford, Preston, Rugby and Bradford had to be profitable in its own right. Each works had to show its overheads added to the basic building costs entailed in the purchase of materials, labour costs and design expenses. These overhead costs were calculated using as a basis the previous turnover and thus increased after a poor year of trading making it extremely difficult to attract business without selling at a nominal cost.

Another repercussion of using this system was that it prevented or delayed improvements to engine design. This was because the extra design costs and overheads had to be added to the selling price of the next batch of engines. This meant that unless there was the prospect of a substantial production run the design work could not be carried out. Some features of English Electric engines, therefore, such as the chain drive for the camshaft, the flat crankcase door, the bevel gear drive for the water and oil pumps, and the less than oil-tight cylinder head covers, were used in English Electric engines long after the designers wanted to replace them.

In the interim, work on the RK vee range of engines proceeded at low budget levels. The aim was to produce the same 2,000bhp from fewer cylinders using the expedient of charge air after cooling. The idea was to use this technique to reduce the overall weight and number of moving parts required in the engine. To achieve this aim would also mean that less turbo-chargers would be required simply because there were fewer cylinders. It was thought within the company that this may well have the effect of increasing reliability.

It is prudent and relevant at this stage to explain technically the limitations of any heat engine deriving power from internal combustion. The amount of power developed by a diesel engine is proportional to how much fuel can be combusted within the cylinders. To burn more fuel involves injecting more air into the cylinders during the induction phase of the engine. Turbo-chargers achieve the aim admirably but the point is eventually reached when they defeat the object, because, as a consequence of compressing the air it inevitably heats and therefore expands. This means that instead of a greater quantity of air reaching the fuel only expanded air reaches it. The solution, therefore, must be to cool the air between the turbo-chargers and the cylinders to overcome and counteract the heating and expansion effect. Also, to avoid the cost of high temperature-tolerant alloys for components having to withstand contact with hot exhaust gases, it is essential to limit the exhaust temperature of the turbo-charger inlets to 600°C. To achieve this entails limiting the air temperature to the cylinder head, thus making aftercoolers doubly required.

Over a two-year period, starting in 1958, English Electric developed the successor of the 16CSVT range featuring the innovation of charge-air aftercooling. Enter into the arena the new 12CSVT engine which was to be fitted into the Class 37s.

Left:
Under a threatening sky, the crew of No 37.178 prepare to leave Perth with the 10.14 empty vans to Manchester (Red Bank) on 2 August 1983. On this occasion, the train numbers 15 vehicles.
Tom Noble

Right:
The 12CSVT power unit is carefully lowered into the completed body shell of a new Class 37 at Vulcan Foundry, Newton-le-Willows, during 1961. Note the 'Deltic' locomotive behind which was under construction at the same time.
Colin J. Marsden collection

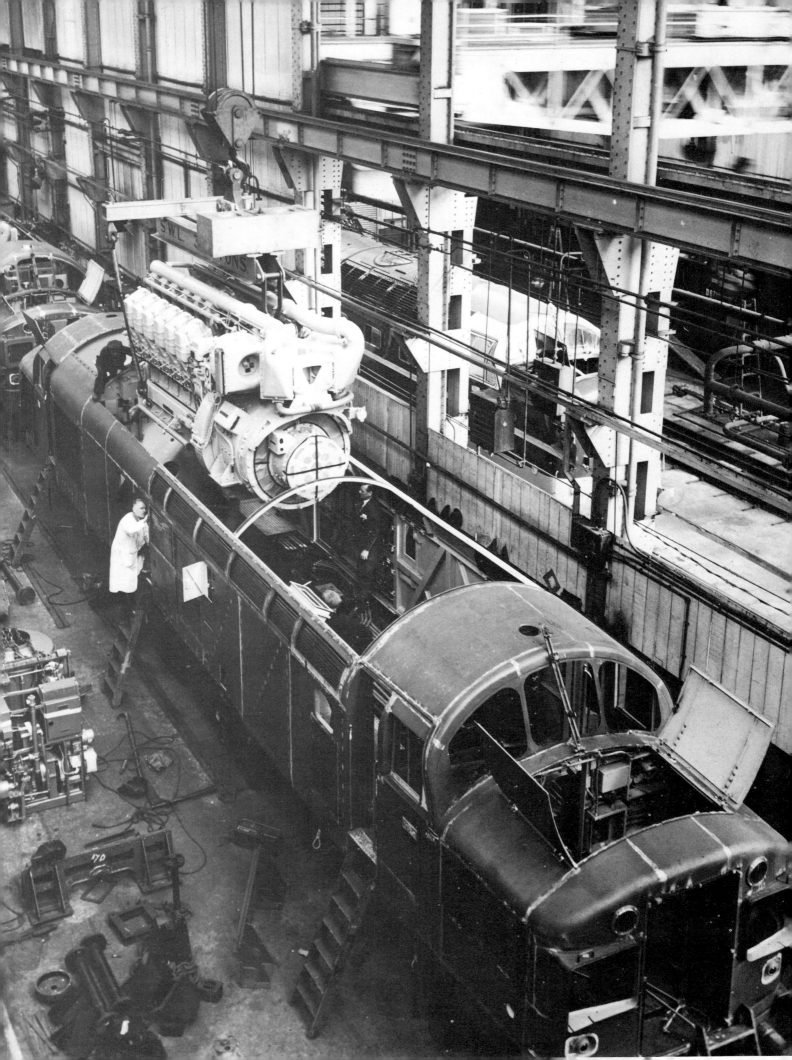

Across the Pennines

SHEFFIELD VICTORIA

Left, top to bottom:
The 14.37 Manchester Piccadilly to Harwich boat train still had the long grinding climb to Woodhead ahead of it when photographed on 3 January 1970. Green-liveried No 6968 was at the front of the train which included a Gresley Buffet (fifth vehicle from the locomotive). *Ian S. Carr*

In pouring rain, No 37.100 (with modified nose end) brings an eastbound oil train into Yorkshire from Lancashire. The bore of Standedge Tunnel can be seen in the distance, but on 17 August 1983, when this photograph was taken, the twin bore on the left had been redundant for many years.
Michael J. Collins

The clean exhaust from No 37.110 indicated that a well maintained machine was at the head of 1M72, the 07.28 Harwich-Manchester Piccadilly as it passed Edale on 20 March 1976. Soon after the photograph was taken this interesting train was diagrammed for haulage by the ubiquitous Class 47s.
Les Nixon

Right, top to bottom:
The station awning at Mythomroyd looks to be in better condition than the battered and redundant signal as No 37.002 leads No 37.168 with a westbound oil train on 27 April 1982. *Les Nixon*

A dismal day, so typical of Pennine locations — No 37.253 passes Diggle with a westbound coal train on 17 August 1983.
Michael J. Collins

The lack of overhead wires, and rusty track, indicates that the Woodhead route had been long closed when this photograph was taken. No 37.083 accelerates into Woodhead Tunnel to pick up a train of lifted track on 15 September 1983. Surely, this was one of the last visits that a Class 37 made to this famous location? *Les Nixon*

3
A Technical
Appreciation

The 12CSVT Engine and its Generators

As described in the previous chapter, it was in 1960 that the 12CSVT engine was unveiled to the public by English Electric. It was a four-stroke machine and the 'C' in the nomenclature referred to 'charge-air cooling'. The engine was rated at 2,025bhp under normal conditions of temperature and pressure, a setting regarded by the manufacturers as the absolute maximum which could be economically developed by the unit. The engine could, of course, be used at a number of settings below this figure. It was a 12-cylinder machine with the cylinders arranged in a 45° formation of the same 10in (254mm) bore and 12in (305mm) stroke of the earlier English Electric diesel motors. In addition the engine was designed to be used at the identical engine speed of 850rpm which the earlier engines utilised. This engine was considerably improved in performance, however. It will be recalled that the first English Electric engine (the 16CSVT Mk I) developed 100bhp per cylinder but the new 12CSVT developed 165bhp per cylinder — an improvement of some 65%.

The new English Electric engine found an immediate application in an order for 10 locomotives designated Class 90 for the East African Railways which were to be used inland from Nairobi on such lines as the 113-mile route to Nakuru and Kisumu. These are arduous and steeply graded lines where poor track makes low axle loadings imperative. These locomotives were of the 1Co-Co1 wheel arrangement and were built at the Darlington factory of Robert Stephenson & Hawthorn Ltd from where they emerged with an axle loading not exceeding 13 tons.

The basic weight of the 12CSVT engine as applied to the East African locomotives — and subsequently the Class 37s — was 32,950lb. This calculates out to a nominal 16.1lb/output horsepower. Peak pressure was quoted at 1,090lb/sq in with a BMEP of 167lb/sq in. Relevant information in relation to the aftercoolers fitted to the engine was that the maximum exhaust temperature was 482°C and the air-to-fuel ratio was 272:1. In order to withstand the higher peak pressure compared to that developed by its predecessors the crankcase had to be redesigned. In addition, the shape of the piston bowl was modified by means of machining it to a less concave, more shallow profile with the aim of gaining an improvement in fuel combustion. Two of the Napier HP2001NT turbo-chargers were fitted to the engine in order to provide the increased boost pressure. Charge-air after cooling was accomplished using a water-cooled heat exchanger unit manufactured by Serck. The fuel racks were controlled by use of a mechanical variable-speed engine governor operating via a gear arrangement which harnessed one camshaft.

The BR Modernisation Plan did not envisage a need for many Type 3s but, after gaining considerable operating experience with the heavy and ponderous English Electric Type 4s (BR Class 40s) and BR/Sulzer 'Peaks', it was decided that a versatile mixed traffic unit was required. This machine, it was decided, should have a good route availability and by implication this requirement demanded acceptable axle loadings. The lighter weight afforded by the 12CSVT engine was the first step in achieving this aim. The 2,025bhp offered from four less cylinders enabled length and therefore weight to be saved and made possible the achievement of a far higher power-to-weight ratio than that made possible by the earlier engine designs.

On 20 November 1960 therefore, the first of the English Electric Type 3 (BR Class 37) locomotives emerged from the English Electric Co's plant at Newton-le-Willows, with the 12CSVT motor installed as its prime mover. The difference between this and the engine fitted to the East African locomotives was that the power unit was at the reduced setting of 1,750bhp. This meant that some 275bhp less was being developed by the engine. It was all that BR considered necessary and the de-rating reduced both peak pressure — to 950lb/sq in — and BMEP — to 145lb/sq in. The consequence of the reduced setting was that it eased the burden of maintenance and the engine was allowed to operate well within its capabilities. The de-rated 12CSVT engine, as fitted to the Class 37s, has the centre line of the power unit shifted by 21in towards number one end for reasons of weight distribution. In service the engine has proved to be highly successful and is certainly the most trouble free of the English Electric power units in the BR traction fleet.

During 1981/82, however, Class 37 No 37.292 was experimentally uprated by engineers at Doncaster Works to produce 2,000bhp. It is understood that the modification was done with a view towards eventually installing an electric train heating generator. This modification would rob some of the traction output from the prime mover and thus reduce the power available at the rail, so the engine has been uprated in an attempt to counteract such a loss. BR have not been keen to divulge the outcome of the experiment but observations indicate that the uprating has had the effect of decreasing the service availability of this particular locomotive.

The 12 cylinders contained in the 12CSVT have cast iron liners, aluminium-silicon alloy pistons, and an alloy cylinder head. The pistons are fitted with five piston rings (three compression rings and two scraper rings). The top compression ring is chrome plated, the second and third are plain cast iron taper-faced compression rings. The pistons are designed to generate a compression ratio of 11.7:1 and the arrangement of the pistons is shown schematically in two groups of six, in Figure 1.

The speed of the engine is controlled pneumatically through the driver's master controller. This means that speed is infinitely variable throughout the engine speed range of 450rpm to 850rpm. The arrangement ensures a smooth control of both the power unit output and of the transition from one power output to another. The main generator field is automatically adjusted by a load regulating device operating at all engine speeds. This is attached to the engine governor in order to match the load to the available engine power — the engine is never allowed to run faster than needed to meet power demand. The obvious advantage is that this device has the effect of keeping fuel consumption to the very minimum. On the Class 37s the load regulators were, for the first time ever on a locomotive supplied to the British Transport Commission, manufactured by English Electric itself. The KV7 load regulators fitted are activated by a hydraulically driven vane motor operated by the governor from the engine oil pressure. If the engine speed of a Class 37 rises above 1,000rpm a mechanically operated overspeed trip comes into operation. This works by shutting down the engine by means of returning the fuel pump racks to the 'no fuel' position. An indication that the device has operated is given by a chrome button which in the untripped mode protrudes from the barrel of the device.

(At this point it is both pertinent and interesting to mention that the English Electric KV10 load regulator was first used on Class 37s. This device was the world famous electronic solid state version which was developed by English Electric technicians. It was ultimately fitted to the successful DP2 diesel prototype and was incorporated into the Class 50 design, but the fact remains that it was experimentally fitted and tested on four Stratford-based Class 37s first.)

Like any complex diesel engine, the 12CSVT is festooned with a multiplicity of pipe work. These pipes are coloured according to their contents using the following code:

white — air pipes
black — drains
light brown — fuel oil
salmon pink — lubricating oil
light orange — conduit
French blue — cooling water

There are two quite separate but interdependent cooling systems fitted into the engine within the Class 37 design. One is for the 12CSVT itself and the other is for the charge-air aftercooler plus the lubricating oil heat exchanger. For both systems coolant is circulated through jackets and radiators by engine driven pumps — one for each system. The cooling group is mounted close to one cab bulkhead, and by definition this is number one end of the locomotive (the radiator end of any BR single-engined diesel is always designated number one end).

Engine cooling is performed by a group of side panel radiators manufactured by Spiral Tube & Components Co Ltd, and also by a roof-mounted fan. Pairs of radiator panels are mounted on each side of the locomotive. The interconnected outer panels cool the water circulating in the two charge-air coolers and the engine lubricating oil cooler, whereas two inner panels are for engine jacket and turboblower cooling. A mechanically driven fan draws air across the radiators and expels it through a roof-mounted grille. The temperature of the jacket cooling water is controlled by a thermostatic radiator by-pass valve.

The whole cooling assembly is enclosed in a sealed compartment situated at the free end of the engine. The 60in Weyroc cooling fan is shaft driven from the engine through a bevel gearbox operating at right angles to the engine. The radiator fan speed is therefore, directly proportional to the speed of the engine. A 'Twiflex' manufactured coupling incorporating a friction clutch is fitted into the vertical drive shaft in order to cushion the drive and reduce the torque imposed on the fans when starting up or shutting down the diesel engine.

Lubrication of the 12CSVT engine uses a wet sump technique and the oil is carried in the sump formed by the engine bed plate. This is provided with filling and draining points and features a dipstick and breather. The 12CSVT needs approximately 120gal of lubricating oil to ensure efficient working.

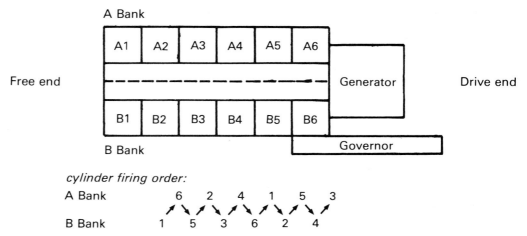

Figure 1:
Schematic representation of Class 37 cylinder arrangement, 12CSVT engine.

cylinder firing order:

A Bank   6   2   4   1   5   3

B Bank   1   5   3   6   2   4

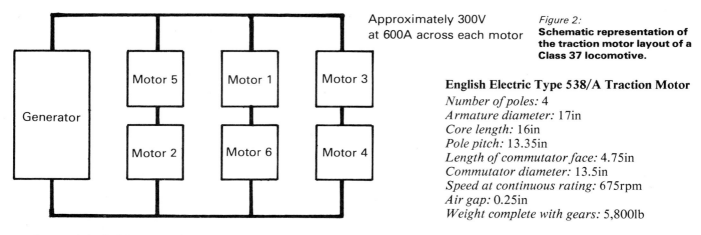

Approximately 300V at 600A across each motor

Figure 2: **Schematic representation of the traction motor layout of a Class 37 locomotive.**

English Electric Type 538/A Traction Motor
Number of poles: 4
Armature diameter: 17in
Core length: 16in
Pole pitch: 13.35in
Length of commutator face: 4.75in
Commutator diameter: 13.5in
Speed at continuous rating: 675rpm
Air gap: 0.25in
Weight complete with gears: 5,800lb

The crankshaft drives a gear-type pump and this draws the oil from the sump and takes it through a coarse strainer to filter off any foreign bodies such as lumps of metal which may be present. The oil is delivered to a cooler which is mounted in 'A' cylinder bank where it is cooled by the water in the charge cooling circuit. If the oil is already cold, a thermostatic by-pass valve allows it to avoid the cooler and flow into the 'Hilco' paper element filters which remove fine impurities. These are arranged in parallel, which means that the oil divides and passes half through each filter. From the filters one branch is taken to the governor and the other to the starting valve and onwards to the main gallery, main and big end bearings, small ends, gudgeon pins, cylinders and ultimately to the crankshaft bearings. The purpose of the starting valve is to restrict the flow of oil to the engine bearings during starting up operations to provide a quick pressure build up to the governor to ensure that the fuel racks open fully.

When the driver selects the EO (Engine On) position on the controller a motor-driven pump runs in order to prime the lubricating oil before the engine is started. When the engine is actually running lubricating oil is circulated by the engine-driven pump at approximately 60lb/sq in, the priming pump having been isolated by an oil pressure operated switch.

Two oil pressure switches are located on the engine. One of these cuts out the motor-driven pump when normal oil pressure is achieved as described above. In the event of an oil pressure failure however, the switch has the additional function of de-energising the engine-run solenoid and thus stops the engine before any damage can take place. The other switch brightens a red oil pressure light on the control cubicle and also the blue fault light in the driving compartment to give warning of oil pressure failure prior to the engine cutting out. The warning operates at 25lb/sq in and the engine stops at 20lb/sq in. Upon receipt of a low oil pressure warning it is imperative, of course, that the locomotive should leave the main line as quickly as possible.

Serck charge-air coolers are fitted between the output side of the blowers and the intake manifold of the engine. They are used to reduce the combustion air temperature and so increase its density in the engine cylinders. This produces an enhanced power output and expedites greater efficiency and fuel economy. The cooled air also helps to cool the piston crown and exhaust valves.

These intercoolers have the effect of raising the temperature of water passing through them by some 2.5°F, from 115°F input water temperature to 117.5°F output temperature. This water circulates through tubes within the cooler, which are manufactured from cupronickel. Water leakage at this point can cause water to enter the cylinders, create a hydraulic lock and cause damage, so it is most important that checks for water leaks on the coolers are carried out regularly.

The main generator fitted to the Class 37s is the dc Type EE822/109, and it is attached to the engine output shaft. It is a self-ventilated, single bearing unit, continuously rated at 1,107kW at 850rpm. In addition to a separately-excited field winding which is used when the locomotive is running normally, it is also fitted with a series field winding which is used when the generator is connected across the battery to facilitate engine starting.

Overhung from the main generator is the auxiliary generator, the Type EE911/5C providing a constant 110V dc for powering the engine support systems. It is a self-ventilating single bearing unit and its output voltage is maintained constant by a carbon-pile voltage regulator manufactured by Newton Brothers of Derby.

Cooling air for both generators is drawn through Airmaze oil-wetted filters fitted next to the machines and set into the sides of the superstructure. The hot air is discharged downwards through the underframe into the atmosphere into prevent recirculation.

Rail traction tests any model of diesel power unit to the absolute maximum, and over the years BR has had to abandon the use of a number of types because traction units have failed to live up to expectations after months of working in a hostile environment. Arduous conditions of vibration and widely varying road characteristics take their toll and some other diesel traction units have had to be de-rated to enable them to cope with the conditions imposed upon them. The problems thrown up by the Sulzer C series engines used in the ubiquitous Class 47s and their subsequent de-rating has been well documented and is quite typical of what is sometimes necessary. By contrast, the English Electric vee-form engine, and particularly the 12CSVT, must be regarded as one of the greatest rail traction prime movers of all time. No English Electric diesel engines have ever been de-rated as a result of inbuilt design weaknesses, and the 12CSVT has stood the test of time. Even after nearly 25 years of exacting BR service, very few Class 37s have to be taken out of traffic through engine problems.

Electrical Equipment and Engine Support Systems
Every diesel-electric locomotive by definition contains within its bodyshell a wealth of electrically operated components needed to derive traction from the prime mover, and the

Class 37 is no exception. Possibly the most significant of the electrical items are the traction motors because it is these which produce movement at the rail.

During 1958 English Electric decided to develop a new four-pole traction motor. It was designed to update the EE Model 526A six-pole motors then being fitted to current building projects such as the prototype 'Deltic'. The new motor, EE model number 538A, sporting a larger diameter axle fitting, was incorporated within the Class 37 locomotive at the design stage. Advantages of the new motor were that it was easier to fit new carbon brushes and commutators and it also had a shorter gear centre and swing radius compared to earlier versions.

The Class 37 has six of these motors which are suspended by the nose and mounted on each driving axle. Each motor, weighing 4,987lb, drives its associated axle by means of a pinion on the armature shaft and single reduction spur gearing with a ratio of 53:19. It is interesting to note that this ratio is exactly the same as both the Class 55 'Deltics' and the English Electric Class 50s. The spur gearing referred to above allows lateral movement of the pinions during operating conditions. The motors are fitted with roller bearing suspension bearers and again are identical with those fitted to the Class 55 'Deltics' with which they were completely interchangeable until the sad demise of the latter class. The use of the same motors in the 'Deltics' — which delivered almost twice the power of the Class 37s — is accounted for by examining the characteristics of the electrical machines used by the locomotive. In Class 37s these operate within their continuous ratings at much lower road speeds than the 'Deltics'. They can carry 600 amps per motor at 13.6mph quite happily without the conductors overheating whilst the generator is operating at its continuously rated current and voltage. Similar treatment of a 'Deltic' at such a low road speed would result in melting of the conductors. The characteristic of Class 37s to produce great power at low load speeds has been referred to elsewhere as 'the low geared effect' though clearly this is nonsense since it has nothing to do with gearing.

The continuous full-field rating of each traction motor fitted to the Class 37 is quoted by the manufacturers as 600 amps at 300 volts giving 222hp at 290rpm. Each group of traction motors is composed of two motors connected in series and the motors are connected in three parallel groups of two in series across the generators (see Figure 2). In normal operation the current across the traction motors should only exceed 2,600amps for extremely brief periods otherwise the overload relay will operate. Similarly, currents between 2,000 and 2,500amps should not be exceeded for more than five minutes once in every hour. A current of 1,800amps should not be exceeded continuously. If a pair of traction motors is cut out for any reason, however, then only two-thirds of the above values apply. The direction of rotation of the motors is reversible and is achieved by reversing the current flow through the motor fields while maintaining the direction of flow through the armature.

The motor fields are arranged for two stages of field diversion, the first at approximately 25mph and the second at approximately 47mph. Each stage is switched on automatically as required by the load regulator. This arrangement allows full engine horsepower to be used over a wide range of locomotive speeds.

The three motors fitted per bogie are force-ventilated by the use of Keith Blackman-manufactured centrifugal blowers situated in the locomotive nose ends. A cramped passageway allows access or entry through to the nose ends from the driving cabs. Each traction motor blower lies to the left of the nose corridor when viewed from the access door in front of the cab. The air is fed from these blowers through a system of ducts and flexible bellow connections to the air inlet at the commutator end of the traction motors. Cooling air is drawn through oil-wetted metal filter panels in the bodyside of the blower compartments.

Wheelslip protection circuits are integrated within the wiring system, which reduces the tendency for wheelslip to occur when power is applied to the road wheels during adverse conditions, such as when rails are greasy or are covered in fallen leaves. Within the circuitry are coupled three wheelslip relays which are sensitive to out-of-balance current between any two of the three motor circuits. In the event of wheelslip being detected these relays initiate three actions: firstly, the amber light in the driving cab is brightened to alert the driving crew of the condition; secondly, the traction motors are prevented from going into weak field; and finally, the engine speed valve is de-energised to return the diesel engine to idling mode in which state the governor will reduce the load to the main generator. Recovery from wheelslip is therefore automatic and requires no action at all from the driver unless is occurs repeatedly. In these circumstances the power handle has to be closed and the anti-wheelslip device operated while notching up.

Compressed air is needed for two main applications on Class 37s. Firstly, it is required for the locomotive braking system which operates through Westinghouse Brake & Signal Co — manufactured 6in × 8in brake cylinders on the bogies. Secondly, air is needed to work the electro-pneumatically operated engine and control gear equipment. Necessary supplies are produced by the 110V electrically driven compressor. Original locomotives were fitted with one Westinghouse Type 2E38/B compressor fitted in number one end. Others of the earlier locomotives were fitted with a Worthington-Simpson compressor — the actual model of compressor fitted varies between batches. At first all locomotives could only haul vacuum-braked stock but later, to enable locomotives to handle trains composed of stock fitted with either train air brakes or train vacuum brakes, some machines were fitted with an additional compressor. This enabled modified machines to cope with the increased demand for compressed air when hauling continuously air-braked rolling stock. These selected machines have been fitted with two of the bigger Westinghouse Type 3VC50 three-cylinder air compressors, both of which are fitted at number one end. Eventually all Class 37s will be fitted with this equipment.

Oil-wetted filters are incorporated into the sides of the locomotives. These are designed to ensure that all air taken into the interior is fully filtered so that all auxiliary equipment, including the air compressors, take air from the filtered supply.

The air supply to the brake system and main reservoirs is maintained at about 100lb/sq in by the compressor governor. The air supply to the straight air brake valves is taken from the straight air supply reservoir which operates via two check valves and a reducing valve set at 80lb/sq in. This arrangement ensures that an air supply is available to operate the brakes in the event of a loss of main reservoir pressure. The two check valves also have the function of giving protection against a burst hose connection between the locomotive body and bogie — no risks can be taken with braking, and 'fail safe' devices must be designed into the system.

Air supply to the electro-pneumatic control gear and also to the engine equipment is reduced to 70lb/sq in.

Although the practice is now being phased out, in the past on BR, Class 37s have been called upon to operate vacuum fitted passenger and freight stock. All of the Class 37s can operate such stock and, indeed, they were originally designed to handle this variety of stock only. During the 1980s BR announced its intention to dispense with vacuum-braked stock and, although such stock will exist for many years, there has been instituted a modification programme aimed at ultimately equipping all locomotives with the extra equipment required to operate air-braked trains in addition to the older vacuum stock. To produce the vacuum required for braking the older stock all Class 37s are equipped with a vacuum exhauster. This is driven by an EE762/4C electric motor from the 110V auxiliary supply harnessed to a Northey flange mounted exhauster. In some individual machines this equipment has been modified by using Reavell exhausters. Coupled within the vacuum system is a vacuum/air proportional valve which ensures that in the event of a train vacuum brake application, there is an automatic proportional application of the locomotive air brakes.

The first batches of locomotives built were equipped with steam heat generating equipment. This was accomplished using a Clayton RO 2500 Mk IV train heating boiler with 2,500lb/hr steam capacity. The actual model of steam generator fitted in the event varied with successive batches. When built, provision was made for removal of the train heating boiler if conversion to electric train heat was thought necessary at a later date. The modification, if fitted, would divert some engine output away from its primary objective of developing electrical energy for traction. British Rail has declared its intention to rid itself of steam-heated passenger stock with some dispatch and if Class 37s are to remain in passenger service an uprating of the diesel engine must be considered. Earlier in the chapter it was mentioned that No 37.292 was uprated to 2,000bhp during 1982. It will be remembered that the 12CSVT engine is fully capable of producing such an output. No electric train heat equipment has been fitted to any Class 37 at this stage but during 1983 BR authorised some 100 machines to be so equipped. This was later amended to cover 31 units only. Latest information suggests that the idea of using a supplementary diesel engine to drive an alternator is being given serious consideration. This would be a way of producing current for the ETH generator, thus obviating the need to uprate, so that the good reliability figures of the de-rated 12CSVT can be retained.

In Class 37s fuel is carried in a 900gal underslung tank which is fitted with a gauge and filling points on both sides of the locomotive. Recently, some class members have had their steam heating equipment removed and the redundant water tanks converted to form additional fuel tanks giving an enhanced fuel capacity of 1,720gal.

A motor driven pump, manufactured by Varley, draws fuel from the tank via a suction strainer and delivers it to the diesel engine by way of a damping vessel, filter, and air separator. Fitted on the separator is a relief valve which allows excess fuel to pass to an emergency fuel tank which will allow gravity feed should the main tank inadvertently run empty or should the fuel-pump fail. A low fuel light is provided on the control cubicle to warn enginemen when the level in the tank has dropped to 50gal. This is operated by float switches in the main tank. Under normal conditions 50gal is sufficient for approximately 30min running. The emergency tank holds 30gal, sufficient for approximately 20min running. When working on emergency fuel, the driver is instructed to treat the situation as a full emergency and the locomotive must, therefore, be driven to the nearest point where it can be taken off the main line.

The Locomotive Superstructure and Bogies

The Class 37 underframe consists of a centre section of two longitudinal joists. These are used to support the 12CSVT engine, fuel tanks, water tanks and also two identical outer sections of two prefabricated members over the bogies. The latter are cross-connected by transoms of welded construction to form the bogie pivot centres, with a number of cross stretchers provided for the purpose of adding strength.

The superstructure side framing is prefabricated and then welded to the underframe. At roof level, removable roof sections are provided over the power unit, control cubicle and boiler to allow ease of access for maintenance or removal of various items of equipment.

The bogies fitted to the Class 37s are identical in all respects to those fitted to the much loved 'Deltics' with which they were completely interchangeable. The design of the bogie can be traced back to that fitted in the prototype 'Deltic' which suffered from a long (14ft 4in) wheelbase. It was designed to negotiate curves of just over five-chains radius and severely restricted the route availability of the 'Deltics'. Clearly, if the bogie fitted to the Class 37s was to allow a true mixed-traffic type to be developed this bogie had to be considerably modified.

Earlier, mention was made of the new design of traction motors fitted to Class 37s. The design incorporated four poles instead of six and gave rise to a shorter swing radius. Also, as a consequence of only three traction motors being mounted on each bogie, a considerable reduction in wheelbase of the bogie could be accomplished. The minimum track curvature that the 61ft 6in length of a Class 37 can negotiate is thus four chains. This compares favourably with that of the prototype 'Deltic' and also the Class 40's 4½ chains.

The prime selling point of the bogies fitted to the prototype 'Deltic' was the section and strength of the bogie transoms and these were retained in the modified bogies fitted to the Class 37s. The shorter wheelbase gave the opportunity to reduce weight and it also afforded the advantage of decreasing the moment of inertia, thus reducing flange forces and track wear.

The 'Commonwealth' pattern bogies fitted to the Class 37s are of the equalised type with swing bolsters. Four side bearers on each bolster distribute the load through four coil-spring assemblies to planks suspended from the bogie frame. The load is then distributed by equalising beams which are underslung-mounted from the axle boxes by four sets of helical springs.

During early 1961 a spate of serious bogie defects began to appear on Class 37s and 'Deltics'. The problem was eventually traced to the rubbing for the transom of the bogie bolster which was found to be coming loose during operation. This resulted in fractures in the vicinity of the traction motor suspension brackets situated on the bogie transom. Remedial work was carried out by English Electric but an inherent fault in the design of the prefabricated bogies made them susceptible to fracture. After research in conjunction with metallurgical experts the fabricated design was abandoned in favour of a cast steel version which was fitted from new on the last 60 Class 37s constructed. Satisfactory modifications were made to the fabricated version, however, and many are still giving sterling service under Class 37s at work today.

An Appraisal

The foregoing material describes the technical features of the Class 37, but how does it compare with its immediate predecessor, the Class 40? There can be no doubt that in the new locomotive English Electric achieved a far better power-to-weight ratio — 1hp to 132lb instead of to 149lb achieved by the Class 40 design. A significant 30-ton difference between its weight and that of the 1Co-Co1 makes the maximum axle load on six axles $17\frac{1}{2}$ tons compared to the Type 4's 18 tons on eight axles. Also, the more compact Co-Co wheel arrangement has the edge over the unwieldy 1Co-Co1 when negotiating track curves. In the context of this the Class 37 is a true mixed traffic design — achieving Route Availability 5 against Route Availability 6 of the older locomotive. The Class 37 can handle most trains that the Type 4 can operate but with the advantage of this superior Route Availability. Imagine a Class 40 being a viable proposition for regular haulage at the top of the Welsh Valleys! The only type of train which the Class 40 should be able to handle with anything like an edge is a long, heavy rake of unfitted freight wagons where its greater bulk and weight can provide better stopping power. However, the new air-braked, fully-fitted freight trains currently being promoted by BR marketing overcome this shortcoming. The Class 37 therefore soldiers on in the face of mass scrappings of its older and more ponderous competitor and, at the time of writing, BR is investigating ways of extending the life of these remarkable machines to enable them to see useful service into the year 2000 and beyond.

Above right:
The removal of the roof hatches allows a good look at the 12CSVT engine in situ. The 10in bore of the cylinders is particularly noticeable in this view. *Ian P. Cowley*

Right:
Class 37 No 37.292 standing in Doncaster Plant on 31 July 1981 where it was undergoing intermediate overhaul. When released for traffic its engine had been uprated to 2,000bhp with a view towards electric train heating (ETH) fitting at a later date. *Barry J. Nicolle*

Left:
No 37.125 (nearest camera) and No 37.300 at Severn Tunnel Junction on 1 June 1983. The large fan, which draws warm air from the engine compartment, is visible from this high viewpoint. The two air-operated 'Desilux' warning horns, fitted to each end of the locomotive, are also visible. *Michael J. Collins*

Below:
A view inside Vulcan Foundry showing English Electric Type 3s under construction. In the locomotive nearest to the camera the traction motor blower has already been installed and the strengthening frames of the superstructure are also evident. The 12CSVT engine waits its turn for fitting in the foreground. Note the 25kV ac electric locomotives under construction on the right.
Colin J. Marsden collection

Top right:
Nothing is left to chance where braking is concerned and this huge train of air-braked vehicles will test the stopping power of No D6968 to the full. The ensemble is standing at Broadholme waiting to take the Westinghouse P4 distributor test train up to Peak Forest.
Westinghouse Brake & Signal Co

Bottom right:
The almost completed body shell of a new English Electric Type 3 is carefully lowered on to its 'Commonwealth' pattern bogie at Vulcan Foundry.
Colin J. Marsden collection

Left:

The new English Electric Type 3s were drafted on to GE line services from new where they took on 'Britannia' Pacific diagrams. In this view 'The Essex Coast Express' is hustled along the Clacton branch near Wivenhoe on 17 July 1962 with No D6782 in charge.
Colin J. Marsden collection

Below left:

The GE area authorities were soon confident enough of their new locomotives to send them off-region on specials. Here, an early visitor to the Southern Region was No D6706 recorded passing Woking with an excursion to the Farnborough Air Show on 13 September 1964.
Brian Stephenson

Below:

When introduced the English Electric Type 3s did an enormous amount of work alongside steam traction. In this view at Carlisle Citadel on 19 August 1963, No D6852 has worked in on a Glasgow–Morecambe extra, while 'Black 5' 4-6-0 No 45349 passes time with another Type 3. *Derek Cross*

GN Main Line

Above:
A splendid photograph of green-liveried English Electric Type 3 No D6814 passing Cambridge Junction, Hitchin with the 16.10 service from King's Cross to Cleethorpes. The superb rake of maroon coaches adds interest to the scene. *Chris Burton*

Above right:
The Type 3s were associated with some crack 'Pullman' services out of King's Cross during the early 1960s. Here No D6800 arrives with the up 'Sheffield Pullman' on 17 May 1965. Note that the numbers were carried at both ends of the locomotive at this time. *Brian Haresnape*

Right:
The Class 37s were soon transferred away from the East Coast main line and in recent years they have made only rare appearances at King's Cross. Bursting out of Hadley Wood tunnel in charge of an unidentified up extra is No 37.097 recorded on 5 August 1981. *Michael J. Collins*

Left:
In recent years there has been a regular freight diagram which takes examples nearly into King's Cross terminus. No 37.170 leans to the curve at Harringey while in charge of the Fen Drayton–King's Cross (Wilments RMC siding) sand train on 25 August 1981. *Michael J. Collins*

On Great Central Metals

Left:
A historic photograph indeed. A green-liveried English Electric Type 3, No D6814, heads green-liveried Southern coaching stock forming the 10.08 York–Bournemouth through train on 11 April 1964, and is seen passing Kirby South Junction. At the time this was the only daytime passenger service remaining on the old GCR main line. *J. Cupit*

Below left:
English Electric Type 3s have never been common at the south end of the Great Central London extension, but on 9 March 1965 No D6749 was captured on film passing South Ruislip with a Sheffield–Wembley Hill hockey international special. *John Faulkener*

Right:
A long coal train heading eastwards, itself on GCR metals but passing under the Midland main line at Wath Junction, on 28 March 1977. The locomotive is No 37.111 and displays in its integral headcode box the four noughts array so typical of this era in BR history. *Gavin Morrison*

Left:
As track maintenance takes place, Clipstone Concentration Sidings, near Mansfield, plays host to a visitor from March in the form of No 37.097 on 10 August 1981. The train is an air-braked freight which has arrived from the Lincoln direction. *Michael J. Collins*

The North East

Left:
The rugged appearance of No 37.059 blends well with the industrial background of Teesside in this scene at Lackenby, Middlesbrough on 21 January 1983. One tank wagon is no match for this 1,750hp machine. Note the shunter's pole wedged in the locomotive buffer — a common North Eastern practice. *Les Nixon*

Below:
A superb photograph of No 37.065 as it prepares to leave the Alcan Lynemouth ship unloading facility with a block load of hoppers at North Blythe, Northumberland on 15 June 1981. The skirting area below the buffers remains unmodified on this machine as photographed. *Geoff Dowling*

Right:
When compared to the previous plate the skirting modification undergone by No 37.016 is obvious. It was photographed leaving Consett Lower Yard with a departure for Tyne Ward on 27 June 1980. *Michael Rhodes*

Above:

A typical working for a North East-allocated machine as No 37.226 leaves Harden Colliery sidings with a vacuum-braked coal train destined for South Bank on 3 June 1983. *Paul D. Shannon*

Right:

No 37.147 snarls round the curve at Newton Hall, Durham with the 23.28 Grangemouth-Haverton Hill hydrocyanic acid train on 14 May 1982. Note the interesting barrier vehicles placed to protect the train crew and guard from the dangerous cargo in the event of an accident.
Paul D. Shannon

GN/GE Joint Line

Right:
The GN/GE Joint Line has, over the years, seen a variety of Class 37 turns on both passenger and freight. On 4 September 1982, the 08.33 (Saturdays Only, Summer Dated) Derby-Great Yarmouth train passes typical Fenland scenery at Pinchbeck in the care of No 37.174.
Michael J. Collins

Below right:
The remains of the goods shed and redundant signalbox make a sad sight at Helpringham, as Gateshead-allocated No 37.087 passes with a Morpeth-Spalding 'Adex' run in conjunction with the Spalding Tulip Parade on 7 May 1983. This locomotive worked the excursion throughout — out and back — stabling the stock at Peterborough.
Michael J. Collins

Below:
On the now closed and lifted section of track, No 37.131 of Healey Mills passes the delightful array of semaphore signals that once existed at French Drove Loop, between March and Spalding. The train is the 10.50 COY Belmont Sidings (Doncaster)-March East Yard sand empties.
Michael J. Collins

Left:
The Doncaster-March East Yard sand train again, but this time rounding the curve into March station on 11 September 1982. The train is formed of PAA sand hoppers and the locomotive is No 37.016 showing clearly the final style of modification for the redundant headcode boxes. *Michael J. Collins*

Air-Braked Freight

Below left:
A number of Class 37s have, since building, been fitted with equipment for braking AB trains, as has No 37.086 illustrated here. It is recorded hammering down the GE main line with a train of VDA vans forming the Chelmsford-York empties, which will be attached to a northbound service at Ipswich Yard.
Michael J. Collins

Right, top to bottom:
Heading east near Barnetby is No 37.127 with a Tyne Yard-Immingham ABN freight on 13 April 1983. This particular machine is well travelled starting its life at Cardiff in May 1963 and seeing subsequent allocations at Newport, York, Gateshead, Thornaby, Tinsley, Saltley, Immingham and Bristol. When photographed the locomotive was operating from Gateshead depot again.
Michael J. Collins

One of the machines reliveried with wrap-round yellow ends, No 37.112 had strayed a long way from its native Scotland when photographed approaching Dringhouses, York on 7 April 1983. The great variety of stock used in the modern air-braked freights makes for interesting trains.
Michael J. Collins

The VEA type four-wheel short-wheelbase vans are often used for military traffic. Some 15 of them are marshalled in this train seen approaching Undy, Severn Tunnel Junction, on 1 June 1983 behind No 37.279.
Michael J. Collins

Above:
When brand new No D6822 had the task of hauling the prototype 'Deltic' from Vulcan Foundry to its final resting place at the Science Museum, South Kensington. Subsequently renumbered No 37.122, the same machine was recorded passing Hampstead Heath at the head of an air-braked working to Temple Mills on 24 July 1980. *Michael J. Collins*

Left:
The Eastleigh-Severn Tunnel Junction ABN service sometimes produces a Class 37 and on 16 October 1981 the photographer was able to record No 37.159 on this duty. The location was Ashley Down Bank, Bristol. *Geoff Gilham*

4
Cosmetics and Liveries

The Recognition Features of the Locomotive Exterior

Externally the Class 37s are very similar to the older Class 40s although when standing side by side the greater length of the latter locomotives is immediately apparent. The Pilot Scheme had given designers a more or less free hand in the aesthetic appearance of their locomotives. In August 1956, however, a BTC design panel was established, but this came too late to have any significant effect on the Class 40s. Outside consultants were called in and they succeeded in tidying up salient features of the detail under the direction of Professor R. D. Russell and these recommendations were carried through and applied to the Class 37s.

The principal change from the Class 40 design was in the mounting of the drawgear on the end of the mainframe rather than on the bogie as had been the case with the earlier design. Within the Class 37 the most obvious detail difference lies in the front end layout. Locomotives numbered D6700-D6818 were constructed with gangwayed connecting doors added in the nose ends with a view to inter-locomotive communication when working in multiple. The machines fitted with this feature are characterised by the split headcode boxes situated one each side of the gangway doors, and the warning horns sited inside round covers which are fitted immediately above the headcode boxes. In recent years, however, some locomotives in this batch have been fitted with the modified front end applied to later locomotives after accident damage has necessitated repairs to the nose.

The headcode boxes were used for displaying a four-character letter and numeral type of headcode which had been devised with the idea of describing various essential items of data about the train for the use of signalmen and other railway personnel. The numbers and letters inserted in the boxes indicated the classification and number of the train and thus aided routeing.

The gangway connection doors referred to above, which formed an important feature of the earlier Class 37s, were in the event rarely used and it became obvious at an early stage that they could be dispensed with. The batch from D6818-D6606 lacked this feature and the opportunity was taken to tidy up the front end appearance of these machines. This was accomplished by mounting the headcode boxes centrally on the nose with the horns being mounted on the roof above the middle driving cab window. Subsequently the authorities received many complaints from footplate staff about the draughty cabs in Class 37s, particularly the batch fitted with end doors. A modification was carried out and locomotives gradually appeared in traffic with the front end doors welded up. A further modification has been to replace the end doors completely with a single piece of sheet steel welded to the front of the locomotive.

During early January 1976 a decision was made to dispense with the headcode displays. This was because they were now an anachronism, being hardly used, particularly with the advent of modern electronic signalling systems. This brought some minor variations. Initially all locomotives worked in traffic with the roller blinds wound round to display four noughts, a convention designed to prevent confusion in the interim period pending a decision as to what solution could be devised for replacement of the redundant headcode boxes. This arrangement was followed by the effective British Rail 'G39' modification. This consisted of a black adhesive panel containing two circular semi-transparent areas which were illuminated by the original panel lights to act as markers. The idea was that this would aid sighting of an approaching train by trackside personnel, particularly at night. More recently, this arrangement has been further modified in a tidying up operation by welding steel plates over the old headcode panels. These plates are painted yellow, and a piece of translucent glass, held in place by rubber grummets, is inserted into the centre. This acts as a window for the headlamps.

An interesting variation on some machines deserves a special mention. Some locomotives which were originally fitted with split headcode boxes have been involved in collisions severe enough to warrant the replacement of the nose end. The replacement has been with central headcode panels so that at least Nos 37.073, 37.074 and 37.091 are in traffic with integral marker lights and boxes. A further variation occurred during early 1983 when No 37.100 and later No 37.006, appeared in traffic with the redundant headcode boxes and gangway doors completely removed. They were replaced with a remodelled front end and neat marker lights similar in appearance to those carried by Class 45 locomotives.

From June 1978, a further modification to the front end of

the Class 37s was instigated. They were made to look yet more like their sister Class 40s by having the lower skirting section of the nose end, from which the buffers protrude, re-profiled under modification No MB235/149. A further detail difference which began to appear in the late 1970s was the replacement of the original large round buffers by a less obtrusive buffer, oval in shape. At the time of writing some machines still retain their original round buffers. At times, locomotives have appeared in traffic with one of each type of buffer on a single front end, making a very peculiar sight.

During the early 1960s No 37.022 appeared in traffic with twin flashing blue headlights attached to the front of the locomotive below the lamp brackets. The experiment was not followed up by a general modification but some of the South Wales allocation were fitted with a single headlight for negotiating ungated crossings on the Central Wales line in the hours of darkness. These were attached to the locomotive with a special bar, itself attached to brackets mounted on the nose end of all later machines. In 1983 it was announced that the Director of Operations required headlights to be fitted to all locomotives capable of working at over 90mph. Under modification No FM6062/006 all Class 37s will have a headlight fitted in due course. Scottish-allocated machines that see service on the Far North line are appearing in traffic with searchlights fitted to the nose. These are causing 'dazzle' problems and some way of dipping or dimming them is being investigated. Radio-telephone equipment is also being fitted to some Scottish-allocated locomotives.

When compared to the earlier Class 40s the bodyside grilles were significantly rearranged. The two sides of the basic Class 37 are mirror image in every detail, except that the nose grilles and one small hatch situated on the roof spoil the effect. A prominent bodyside variation involves the radiator air intakes at number one end. When delivered to BR from the makers this area was made tidy by fitting a wire mesh arrangement over the whole assembly, flush with the bodyside. Service experience over the years indicated a measure of undercooling and as a response to this, removal of this wire mesh was begun in the mid-1970s. It was done in order to maximise the air flow across the radiators, and was first started on the Eastern Region, with the Scottish Region following suit shortly afterwards. The WR did experiment with a redesigned grille made from sheet steel with a large pattern of large round holes drilled into it and this region, at least seems to be continuing in the use of the grilles. At the time of writing BR technicians are investigating the modification and the ER is providing technical justification for the removal of the grilles.

Slung beneath the locomotive between the bogies are two large box-like appendages. At number one end this is the fuel tank and the other is the 800gal boiler water tank. Many locomotives, particularly those built without boilers, have had their water tank converted to a second fuel tank, thus increasing their range. At one time such locomotives were identifiable by the addition of a blue spot painted underneath the running number, but this practice now appears to have ceased.

Liveries

The first 19 locomotives were delivered from the makers in plain British Railways standard green. The locomotive body was painted this colour throughout, including the nose ends, and with none of the decorative embellishments such as the lining at shoulder level found on the Class 40s. The bogie sides and underframing were finished in black with red bogie fronts, buffer beams and buffer stocks. Numbers were carried below each cab window and small cast builders' plates were affixed above each number. The BR 'lion and wheel' totem was carried off-centre towards number two end cab.

Small yellow warning panels painted on the lower parts of the noses were soon introduced and these were carried by Nos D6720 onwards when delivered new from English

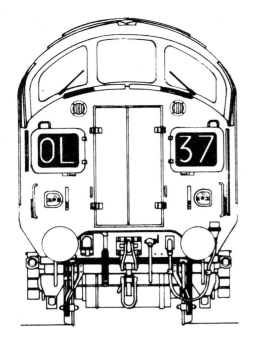

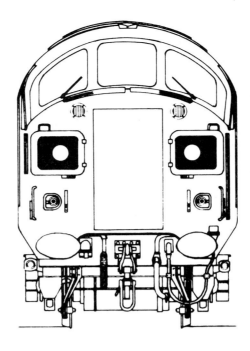

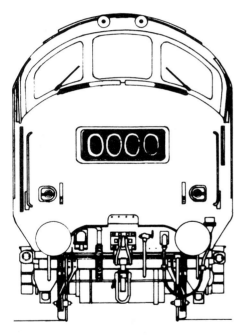

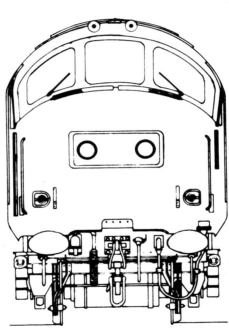

Left:
Front end arrangement of twin headcode box-fitted Class 37 before and after removal of the headcode roller blinds. Note that the warning horns are fitted in the circular grilles above the boxes and note also the distinctive and untidy gangway connecting doors carried by early members of the class. *Graham Fenn*

Below left:
Later deliveries of Class 37 had the front end redesigned to a neater more functional appearance when the gangway doors were found to be unnecessary. The headcode boxes and the marker lights associated with the modern era were mounted centrally on the nose. The 'Desilux' two-tone horns were repositioned above the cab windows at roof level. *Graham Fenn*

Overleaf, top to bottom:
Side elevation of a twin headcode box-fitted English Electric Type 3 with number one end situated to the left. The original numbers were carried one at each end with the BR 'Lion & Wheel' emblem positioned amidships towards number two end. *Graham Fenn*

Plan view of a twin headcode box-fitted Class 37 showing access doors on the roof to expedite engine removal, and similar doors on each nose end for easy removal of traction motor blowers. *Graham Fenn*

Side elevation of a central headcode box-fitted BR Class 37 with number one end situated towards the right. The TOPS numbers are carried on one end only with the BR 'double arrow' logo occupying the same position as the old emblem. Note that the radiator and air intake grilleing is almost a mirror image of the other side of the locomotive, and note also that this grilleing has been removed from the square radiator intake panel, following recurrent cooling problems. *Graham Fenn*

Left:
An English Electrics works photograph of No D6713 taken at the Vulcan Foundry. *English Electric*

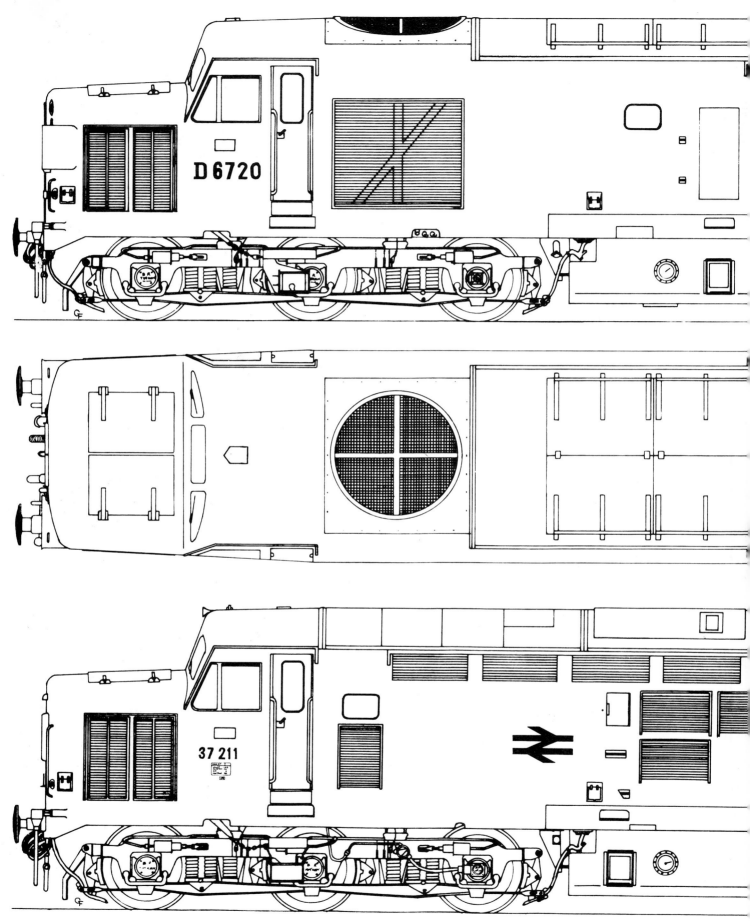

D 6720

37 211

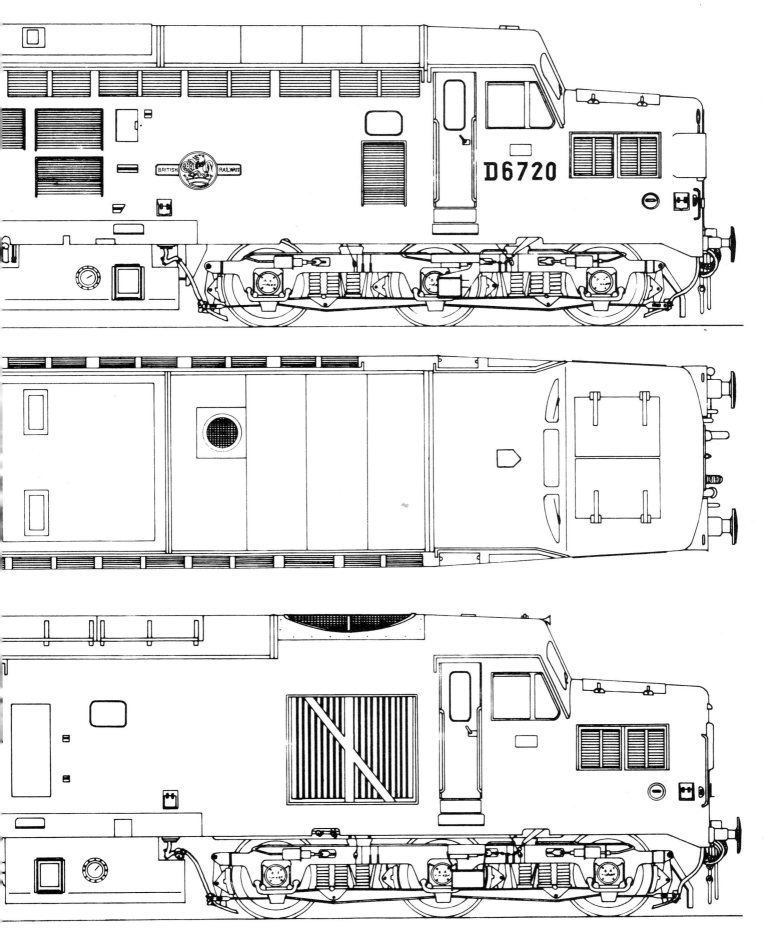

Electric. These were intended to improve visibility of all BR diesels from the trackside. This was later extended to cover all of the nose area with a slight wrap-round on the nose top and sides.

From 1966 BR adopted the new all-over blue livery with large yellow ends. Some Class 37s remained in traffic in green livery for many months until maintenance requirements dictated a works visit and overhaul when machines were repainted. At this time the new 'reversed arrow' logo was applied, some machines getting this in the position on the bodyside once occupied by the old totem, whilst others received their logo underneath the running number. The number style in blue initially remained the same but this was later changed to the present characters with rounded and slightly more legible numbers.

In 1968 the final withdrawal of steam traction from BR (on standard gauge at least) meant that a new classification scheme could be devised. Each class was allocated a number by which it could be identified and the English Electric Type 3s became BR Class 37 — top of the Type 3 power category. Locomotives then began to appear in traffic without the 'D' prefix. At first this was simply painted out, sometimes very untidily, but the situation was gradually smartened up. At this time a small data panel transfer began to be affixed below the numbers giving essential information about the locomotive.

The class number, referred to above, which was allocated to each running type, was later adopted to form the basis of a new number scheme. This was carried out to ease the identification of a particular locomotive by the new TOPS (Total Operations Processing System) then being adopted by BR. This is a real time computer system adopted as an aid to the achievement of greater efficiency. All diesel and electric locomotives began to be renumbered during autumn 1973 and the scheme was applied to Class 37 in such a way as to almost preserve the numerical continuity in the new as in the old numbers. No D6701 became No 37.001, etc, the only exception being No D6700 which became No 37.119; it took the place of No D6819 to mark the end of the twin headcode box batch. No D6819 became No 37.283 because No D6983 had already been withdrawn and cut up following accident damage. The 'odd' locomotives, ie Nos D6600-D6608, thus

became incorporated within the overall numbering system, the whole class of 308 surviving machines becoming Nos 37.001-37.308.

Meanwhile livery variations have continued. During summer 1981 two Class 37s, Nos 37.027 and 37.112, appeared decked out in an experimental livery. These two Scottish-allocated machines were seen in traffic with wrap-round yellow ends and black window surrounds. There were, however, slight differences between the detail finish of the two machines. On No 37.027 the yellow area included the cab doors, but on No 37.112 these were excluded. A further stage was reached when, at the end of 1983, No 37.025 emerged from Doncaster Works decked out in the complete new livery previously reserved for Class 50 refurbished units and some Class 56s. Wrap-round yellow ends, black window surrounds, a huge BR logo and outsize running numbers were all featured.

During the late 1970s and early 1980s BR developed a new attitude to locomotive naming, at last recognising the good publicity and increased public awareness that such gestures can generate. During spring 1963 nameplates had been fitted to three of the class commemorating East Anglian regiments but these were never unveiled to the public and were hastily removed by autumn 1963 when the regiments themselves were disbanded. Thus it was left to No 37.180 to be the distinguished recipient of the first nameplate to be carried in public by a Class 37 when it received the bi-lingual nameplate *Sir Dyfed/County of Dyfed* at a ceremony held at Carmarthen station in mid-1981. Later No 37.207 was named *William Cookworthy* after the discoverer of china clay deposits in Cornwall. This was followed by the Scottish Region decision to name five of its allocation after local lochs, perpetuating the theme started by certain Highland Railway and LNER steam locomotive classes. These Class 37s were named at special ceremonies and at this time the custom of painting a small Highland Terrier motif on the bodyside of Scottish-based examples was started. The trend of experimental livery variations continued with the appearance, in 1983, of examples appearing in traffic with a customised white line painted along the bodyside just above sole bar level.

Left:
An early picture of English Electric Type 3 No D6716 at Liverpool Street on an express from Norwich. The split headcode boxes, fitted to the first 119 examples, are very clear in this picture. *Colin J. Marsden collection*

Top:
When the headcode boxes were made redundant in the mid-1970s the letters and numbers in them were wound round to display four noughts. Showing this convention, No 37.112 pauses at Sheffield Midland on 12 January 1978 with a rake of steam-heated Mk I carriage stock. *Michael Rhodes*

Above:
The first solution used in an attempt to tidy up the redundant headcode boxes was to convert them into marker lights by the use of black plastic and a translucent material. No 37.088 shows this modification as it crosses the fens with the 09.35 King's Lynn-Liverpool Street. *Michael J. Collins*

Right:
This head-on view of No 37.043 at Cambridge shows the final solution adopted for the headcode boxes. Sheet steel has been attached to the boxes and glass fitted with rubber grummets, to act as marker lights. This gives a fairly tidy appearance. *Michael J. Collins*

Above:
The low winter sunlight illuminates the skirting modification on No 37.075 as it passes Manea in 7° of frost with a Peterborough-Thornton Fields empty vans working on 7 January 1982.
Michael J. Collins

Left:
The twin blue flashing headlight modification fitted to No D6722 photographed on 2 August 1966. The experiment was not considered successful enough to be continued.
David L. Percival

Right:
In original green livery without yellow warning panels, No D6790 leaves Kingmoor Yard, Carlisle with a freight for Newcastle on 10 June 1967. The brake tender, coupled behind the engine, was often attached during the 1960s to give extra braking power when hauling long unfitted freights.
Derek Cross

Below:
Intended to improve visibility of an approaching train for those engaged in work by the trackside, the English Electric Type 3s were painted with a small yellow warning panel. Watched by a small boy, No D6701 passes Godley Junction, under 1,500V dc wires, when heading the 14.42 Manchester Piccadilly to Harwich train during September 1966. *F. Wilde*

Far left:
Painted in blue with full yellow ends and the BR 'double arrow' logo situated beneath the running number, No D6889 passes Pontypridd with a freight from Merthyr on 21 August 1968. *Phillip Fowler*

Left:
The data panel as attached to No 37.011. Also visible is the Vulcan Foundry workplate situated just above the running number. *Michael J. Collins*

Below left:
With wrap-round yellow ends, black window surrounds and number situated on the body side panelling towards number one end, No 37.112 sparkles in the spring sunshine as it heads away from Tyndrum Lower station on 13 April 1982. The working is the 12.54 Glasgow (Queen Street)-Oban service. *Les Nixon*

Below:
The final livery scheme. The first locomotive to be repainted with full yellow wrap-round ends, black window surrounds, large numbers and giant BR logo was No 37.025, photographed at Doncaster Works in December 1983. *Derek Porter*

Bottom:
The nameplate of No 37.027 *William Cookworthy* is clearly visible in this view of the machine at Drinnick Mill, Cornwall on 29 July 1983. The train consists of Tiger Rail Leasings' china clay wagons. *Michael Rhodes*

47

Left:

Sir Donald Cameron of Locheil, the Lord Lieutenant of Inverness-shire, gives a short speech after naming No 37.027 *Loch Eil* at a ceremony at Glasgow (Queen Street) on 6 October 1981. Mr Leslie Soane, General Manager of BR Scotland, looks on. The highland terrier motif, applied to some Scottish based machines, is clearly visible. *Tom Noble*

Below:

No 37.043 *Loch Lomond* passes the Forth & Clyde canal near Knightswood North Junction while in charge of the 12.55 Glasgow (Queen Street)–Oban on 30 April 1983. *Tom Noble*

Lancashire Hotpot

Below:

The summer Saturday trains from Blackpool to Sheffield have become well-known Class 37 workings in recent years. Framed in the road overbridge, No 37.122 approaches Poulton-le-Fylde with the 13.53 (Saturdays Only, Summer Dated) service to the steel city on 14 August 1982. The haulage fans, situated in the front coach, have become a characteristic feature in recent years of trains which can produce a locomotive normally used on freight diagrams.
Geoff Dowling

Right:

Some Tinsley-based locomotives have been receiving unofficial '41A' shedplate stickers reminiscent of the steam age and applied by enthusiasts. This is evident above the vestibule doors on No 37.046 photographed negotiating Farrington Curve, south of Preston, while heading the 13.59 (Saturdays Only, Summer Dated) Blackpool–Sheffield on 30 July 1983.
Steve Turner

Top left:

A Newcastle-Manchester (Victoria) relief formed of Mk I coaches hauled by No 37.090 had just passed Diggle Junction when recorded on 13 April 1982. Such clear conditions as this are rare in Pennine locations.
Steve Turner

Bottom left:

The line over Copy Pit from Burnley to Todmorden sees very little passenger traffic. It does however come briefly to life on summer Saturdays to allow passage of trains to Sheffield from the Lancashire coast. The 13.59 (Saturdays Only, Summer Dated) Blackpool–Sheffield train is seen passing Portsmouth on 27 August 1983 with No 37.126 in command.
Les Nixon

Engineers' Trains

Right, top to bottom:

Taking a westward ballast train out of Llantrisant sidings is an unkempt No 37.255 on a cloudy 2 June 1983. Class 37s are ideal for such trains having immense power at low speeds and are, therefore, a favourite choice for engineers' department trains in South Wales and elsewhere. *Michael J. Collins*

The telephoto lens accentuates the gradient as No 37.039 brings a train of nine 'Seacows' into Colchester from the Ipswich direction on Sunday 26 September 1982. The branch to Clacton can be seen diverging on the right.
Michael J. Collins

A sylvan setting for No 37.175 as it ambles through Frampton Mansell, on the Gloucester-Swindon line, with a load of ballast on 15 May 1982. Hopefully, the snow ploughs were not required again that year!
Geoff Dowling

Top left:
The Blue Star multiple working code allows No 37.197 to doublehead with Class 31 No 31.311 on a lengthy train of rail. The pair are seen approaching the weed infested platforms at Elmswell, Suffolk on 20 August 1982.
Michael J. Collins

Bottom left:
Joining the river of freight on the South Wales main line is this engineers' special hauled by No 37.239. It was seen emerging from the twin tunnels at Gaer Junction, west of Newport, on 1 June 1983. *Michael J. Collins*

Car Carriers

Right, top to bottom:
Motorail trains always make interesting subjects for photography and one from the south arrives at Inverness on 31 August 1982 behind No 37.262 — one of the boilered batch newly transferred from Stratford. Already it has received its headlight situated above the integral marker light box.
Kim Fullbrook

Throbbing along the Harwich Branch near the former station at Bradfield is No 37.259 in charge of the 14.10 Harwich (Parkeston Quay)-Paisley ABN freight. On this occasion, 23 February 1983, it consisted of a loaded set of 'Cartics'.
Michael J. Collins

A rather travel weary No 37.038 seems to be making heavy work of the 14.10 Parkeston Yard-Mossend ABS freight. The missing grilles from the radiator intake are easily apparent — a measure taken in an attempt to improve air flow and combat cooling difficulties. *Michael J. Collins*

53

Bridge Crossings

Far left:
Three Mark Is are a mere plaything for No 37.112, photographed crossing the Caledonian Canal outside Fort William with a late afternoon train for Mallaig on 27 July 1981. *Kim Fullbrook*

Left:
No 37.081 makes a fine sight as it heads the Sighthill-Fort William ABS freight over the bridge at Dumbarton on 1 June 1981. The water below drains Loch Lomond and allows its cool waters passage to the Irish Sea. *Brian Denton*

Below:
No 37.112 again, but this time crossing the Horseshoe Bridge while powering the Fort William-Mossend freight on 28 August 1981. The desolate, windswept, barren and lonely nature of the countryside is emphasised in this view. Certainly not an easy place to run trains in the winter time, and a locality where the slow speed power of a Class 37 will be appreciated *Kim Fullbrook*

Left:
Crossing the River Don by a splendid girder type bridge on the Doncaster avoiding line is No 37.208, heading a rake of mineral hoppers on 15 August 1975. The bridge beyond once carried the one-time Hull & Barnsley and Great Central Joint Railway . *Terry Flinders*

Bottom left:
Shooting against the light has produced an image of some impact. A novel silhouette has been produced accentuating the delicate water pattern of the River Blythe near Kittybrewster as an unidentified Class 37 passes on a coal train on 15 June 1981. *Geoff Dowling*

Coal Trains

Right, top to bottom:
Heavy coal trains are the Class 37s' forte because their great power available at slow speeds can be utilised to the full. Threading the Hope Valley and the Derbyshire hills is No 37.253 heading a westbound Mansfield-Garston Docks coal train near Goale on 12 August 1983. *Steve Turner*

A busy scene at Healey Mills, Wakefield. A mixed freight headed by a brace of Class 20s works into the yard and passes No 37.197 leaving with a vacuum-fitted coal train on 6 April 1983. *Michael J. Collins*

No 37.126 seems to be working hard as it approaches Knottingly station on a rake of coal empties on 7 April 1983. This line sees an immense amount of coal traffic to the power stations on the lower River Aire, but more usually in merry-go-round mode in the hands of Class 56s. *Michael J. Collins*

Left:
No D6999 was the 300th English Electric Type 3 to be constructed and was delivered for service during October 1965. In this photograph the locomotive is seen on its very first working in revenue earning service, hauling a block load of coal to Llanwern steelworks.
English Electric

Below left:
The combined 3,500hp of two Class 37s is more than enough to keep this set of HAA MGR hoppers on the move when empty. The pair were photographed on 18 August 1983 traversing the ex-Midland Erewash Valley main line at Bennerley Junction, Ilkeston. The bridge used to carry the ex-GNR line to Derby Friargate.
Michael J. Collins

Below:
The overhead catenary at Wath for the use of the Woodhead route electrics was still in place when this photograph of No 37.019 was taken on 11 August 1981. The Stratford based machine was about to head west with a loaded train of MGR hoppers. *Michael J. Collins*

Right:
Industrial desolation and decay as No 37.241 waits at Aberbeeg, South Wales, with empties for Rose Heyworth Colliery. The yards on the right were once a thriving freight centre but their rotting remains now present a very sad picture. *Paul D. Shannon*

5
The Driver's View

Like any large and complex organisation with diverse human interaction, BR must have an extremely rigid set of rules, instructions and procedures to be followed by all employees and operatives. The BR driver is no exception and he must learn, understand and be able to recall a plethora of rules which are applicable to his day-to-day life. Signalling, emergency procedures, safety precautions, route knowledge, and traction procedures are all aspects of the driver's activities and he must know the rules and instructions which apply to each and every activity he undertakes on duty. It may come as no surprise, therefore, that the driver of a Class 37 must follow a strict code of practice whilst carrying out the apparently simple task of preparing a Class 37 to fulfil its rostered duty.

The first part of this chapter is meant to give the reader a driver's eye view of the duties which must be performed on a dual-braked Class 37 before using the machine in traffic. For the purpose of this article it has been assumed that the locomotive has been standing for more than three hours after it has been immobilised by the performance of full disposal duties by the previous train crew.

On arrival at his rostered locomotive, the driver must first enter the driving cab to deposit his personal belongings and also take the opportunity of ascertaining that the handbrake has been applied. Having done this he then climbs down from the machine and commences an external examination of the locomotive to ensure that there are no obvious defects such as damage to the fuel and boiler water tanks, or any missing or damaged parts of the bogies. At the driving end he must ensure that no red flags or 'not to be moved' markers are displayed and check that all hoses are stowed in their correct dummy plugs or brackets and that their operating cocks are closed. At this point he is encouraged to check that the steam heat pipe (where fitted) is secured on its chain and check that the vacuum hoses are seated on their dummy plugs. At the same time he must ascertain that the blue star multiple control jumper cables fitted to his locomotives are secure and safe with the protective covers fitted to the sockets.

The driver is then urged to proceed in a clockwise direction round the locomotive to perform a series of safety checks. He must ensure that there is sufficient sand in the sandboxes to cover the perceived requirements of the rostered duties and then check that there are no external cables or pipes which might snag or break as the locomotive moves off.

When a locomotive is to be stabled for some time, wedge-shaped chocks or wheel scotches are placed next to the wheels to prevent the machine from running away. All these must be removed before an attempt is made to move the loco-

motive. Having accomplished this, the driver must then check that the glass is not broken over the fixed fire extinguisher external operating handles. Still proceeding round the locomotive in a clockwise direction he must move the lighting change-over switch to the 'Battery' aspect and check the main fuel and water tank gauges which are situated underneath the locomotive superstructure just below sole bar level. Continuing on his way the driver must now check that the main fuel isolating cocks are open and that the boiler fuel cock is open when it is likely to be required. He must then turn his attention to the boiler water tank gauge and check that there is sufficient water to supply the boiler to generate steam for the train heating. As steam-heated carriage stock disappears into history it is likely that these boilers will be removed completely from Class 37s, therefore making the duty referred to above superfluous.

On his way round the locomotive the driver must always be mindful to look out for obvious defects which can be spotted by even a cursory examination, such as leaking fuel or water. Having accomplished the tasks referred to above, the driver is then supposed to enter the driving cab and complete checks on the brake gear by ensuring that the locomotive automatic brake valve is at the shutdown position and check that the straight air brake valve is at the 'off' position. Various other safety checks have to be made in the cab area including monitoring the detonator case, checking that a red flag is carried, and ascertaining that track circuit operating clips are present as outlined in the BR rule book. At this time the driver is also urged to check the cab fire extinguisher and the AWS cut-in equipment, and ensure that the repair book is present in the cab area.

Still in the driving cab the driver must then turn the brake selector switch to the 'air passenger' aspect, check that the main boiler switch is set at 'off' (where this machinery is present in the locomotive) and check that the miniature circuit breakers and exhaust switches are set at 'on'. At the same time he must make sure that all other switches are set at their normal positions, that the earth fault relay is not tripped and that spare fuses are available in the event of them being required.

The fuel capacity of a Class 37 fitted with standard fuel tanks is about 920gal of diesel fuel and it is the driver's responsibility to ensure that there is sufficient fuel present in the tanks to fulfil the duty for which the locomotive is rostered. Similarly the boiler water capacity is 800gal and the driver, or his assistant, must ensure that sufficient water is available to heat the steam-heated carriage stock for all of the journey if a passenger duty is included within the work diagram. Fire is an ever-present hazard on any diesel locomotive and so the traction authorities regard it as an important aspect of the driver's preparation to remove the safety pins from the Carbon Dioxide fixed fire extinguishers before starting the locomotive. For the same reasons he must check that the cab cooker hotplate has not been left switched on inadvertently by the previous crew.

At this point the driver is urged to proceed to the non-driving cab by way of the internal passageway which leads through the engine compartment. Whilst passing through that area he must check the main fuel gauge. The water level in the radiator header tanks and the cocks in the fuel supply to the engine should also be checked for correct setting. English Electric engines are fitted with a governor over-riding lever and the driver must ascertain that this lever is set at the top of its quadrant and finally check the battery isolating switch which is also situated in the same general area. When he ultimately reaches the non driving-cab the driver must perform all the safety checks carried out in the first end, and in addition must press the fire alarm test button, and hear the bell ring, to make absolutely sure that the system is working.

The driver then inserts the master key into the controls and moves the master switch to EO (Engine Only). A motor driven lubricating oil priming pump runs when the reverser handle is at 'Engine Only' and the engine is not running. Thus the lubrication system is primed before starting and the driver should leave this handle at EO for 90 seconds prior to pressing the start button. The driver then starts the engine. When a pressure of 95lb/sq in registers on the main reservoir gauge, the automatic brake valve must be moved to the 'running' position and a check made that 70-72lb/sq in is registering on the brake pipe gauge. With the same control the driver then moves the automatic brake valve to the 'initial' position and a check made that the brake pipe pressure falls to 63-65lb/sq in. The automatic brake valve must then be moved in steps to the 'full service' position and a check made that the brake pipe pressure falls to 44-48lb/sq in and that the brake cylinder pressure conversely rises with each step to reach a maximum at the 'full service' position. The automatic brake valve is then set to the 'emergency' position and the driver proceeds to check that the brake pipe pressure falls to zero with the brake cylinder pressure remaining at maximum. This check finally completed, the automatic brake valve is set to the 'running' position.

The checking routine then turns to the straight air brake valve and this is moved to the 'on' position to ensure that the brake cylinder pressure rises to its maximum. This completed the valve is turned to 'off'. With the brake pressure at 70lb/sq in the master switch is turned to the 'for' position and without the DSD (driver's safety device) pedal depressed the driver checks that the brake pipe pressure commences to fall to zero after a three to five-second interval. This completed the automatic brake valve is moved to the 'emergency' position and after a short pause is moved to 'neutral'. The driver then has to move the master switch to 'off' and then remove the master key from the control, leaving the engine running. At this point he changes the brake selector switch to 'vacuum passenger', checks that the battery ammeter is not registering a current discharge and that the fault panel indications are normal. He then releases the parking brake in the cab, switches the red tail lights on, checks that the brake pressure is holding steady and before leaving this end of the locomotive switches the cab lights off and checks that all cab doors and windows are closed.

The driver then proceeds back through the engine compartment and carries out certain checks of a minor nature on the way to the driving cab. He still has to repeat the procedure carried out in the non-driving cab regarding brake and DSD check. All checks completed, the driver can then move off with the locomotive. It must be remembered, of course, that before any driver can prepare a Class 37 for duty he must be passed out to drive the class by being successful in a number of stringent tests.

The cab layout on Class 37s is very similar to that on most of the English Electric diesels delivered before the advent of the Class 50s in 1967. The driver's position is on the left as is customary on British Rail. At his left hand are situated both brake controls. The direct air brake valve operates the locomotive brakes only, whilst the main brake valve causes the simultaneous application of both the locomotive and train brakes.

The power controls are situated at the driver's right hand, and on the master controller console are situated both power and reverser handles, which are mechanically interlocked. The master controller can only be operated with a master key. Between the brake and power controls are arranged a group of five gauges on the instrument panel. These are the air brake gauge, vacuum gauge, main reservoir gauge, main ammeter and the speedometer. Above these are situated below the window, the windscreen wiper controls and the warning lights for wheelslip detection, engine stopped, and fault. To the right of these, behind the master controller console, is the AWS indicator disc and reset, together with switches for standing, engine starting and engine stopping. At foot level, underneath his seat, is the 'dead mans treadle', DSD, which must be depressed at all times the locomotive is in motion.

The right hand side of the locomotive cab houses the seat for the assistant driver or secondman, in front of him, just below window level, are the handbrake wheel, water tank gauge, boiler indicator light and steam pressure gauge. Both of the driving positions are fitted with a valve for operating the compressed air-operated audible horn.

The previous paragraphs have been a description of the drivers' duties and an insight into the complexities of the cab areas. It would be interesting to know what enginemen think of the Class 37s. To evaluate this point the author spent a convivial evening in the company of two Ipswich men who had known the class since its inception. Mr George Baker has recently retired after 48 years of railway service. He started his career at Ipswich and, after spells of duty at Woodford Halse, war service in the Royal Engineer's railway operating department where he served on the Trans-Arabian Railway, he returned to Ipswich for good in 1946. He is a man who obviously loved the railway and remembers with fondness the days of steam on Great Eastern lines. During 1958 he became an instructor for driver training on the then new English Electric Type 4s (BR Class 40s) but in 1960/61 he began instructing on the 1,750hp Class 37s.

The other driver's christian name is Charlie but he prefers his surname not to be divulged so I accordingly adhere to his wishes. Again, he is a warm Suffolk character who has seen very many years of railway work. He first became acquainted with Class 37s when he was sent to Ilford training school for a conversion course on D6700. He was in fact shown the ropes by George Baker and the two men have known each other for years.

These two men have worked on Class 37s on all the routes

known by Ipswich crews — from Ipswich to Liverpool Street, Felixstowe, Peterborough, March (Whitemoor), Norwich, Yarmouth (both via the present lines and the now closed East Suffolk route), Temple Mills, Cambridge, and the Lowestoft-Norwich line. Although they did have to drive other traction units, Ipswich has been associated with Class 37s since 1960 and between them they must have amassed thousands of man-hours service experience on the class.

Straight away both men said that the Class 37s were 'the most noisy, uncomfortable but totally reliable engines on British Rail'. Neither of them had failed on the road badly enough to prevent further progress. Why are the machines so uncomfortable? The answer is that the cabs of English Electric locomotives fitted with nose ends are notoriously cold and draughty. This is particularly so in those fitted with gangway doors which were used to allow access between locomotives when running in multiple. Both men hated this feature and they spoke of an occasion when a time-and-motion expert came down to the depot with his stopwatch to see these end doors in operation. New machines always arrived with these vestibules done up and stuck up with paint and the new machine selected for the experiment was typical. The stop watched was started and two beefy characters set to work to show him what they could do. They heaved and strained, kicked, bashed and swore, but the doors remained stubborn! The time-and-motion man went away, watch still ticking, and returned some while later. The two men worked with a will and after 70 minutes the doors sprang open! The expert was not impressed! George and Charlie went on to describe how on the occasions that they did go through these vestibule doors they would come out stinking because the leather bellows which clipped together to make the connection were swamped with 'neatsfoot oil' — a leather preservative and softener made from certain unmentionable parts of oxen! Another aspect of the gangway vestibules disliked by the men was that if the blower motor — readers will recall that this is situated in the nose — was badly maintained or if the blower air intake was blocked, it would draw air in through the cab. This would sometimes pull the internal doors open and create a terrible draught. Apparently the number one (fan) end was most susceptible to this peculiar fault.

Cabs in Class 40s were heated by the use of warm water from the cooling system, the heated air being drawn into the cab by a fan. These were terribly inefficient, however, and the whole class was modified with electric heaters. The lessons learned were applied to the Class 37s and they were fitted with Cressall-manufactured four-element, 110V cable heaters operating off the auxiliary supply. These were much more effective and the draught problem has been partly resolved by plugging air entry points with polystyrene packing. Many units are now approaching 25 years old and therefore door and window fittings are becoming badly aligned, contributing to the draught problem. Despite the fact that the vestibule doors are redundant and most are now welded up, both enginemen agreed that Class 37s are still very draughty machines to work on, particularly in inclement weather.

As to actually driving the Class 37s both men liked them because they gave a good solid ride. They both agreed that driving techniques must not be too heavy handed because on Class 37s 'everything comes in large lumps'. Here they meant that only two stages of field weakening sometimes gave rise to problems. George recalled the days when heavy loose-coupled freights were taken from Whitemoor over the undulating road to Ipswich. These were meant to run at about 45mph — the worst speed of all for Class 37s because they keep banging in and out of weak field making extraordinary noises. In Suffolk parlance I am told that this behaviour is known as 'lumping about'. Very descriptive! Both men said that on passenger trains — particularly when hauling eight or nine bogies out of Liverpool Street — they were seriously underpowered and were not masters of the work. Charlie mentioned how, when working the 16.50 down out of Liverpool Street which followed a slow train, they would often get checked at Gidea Park. The large gap between the first and second stage of field weakening would often give rise to problems in accelerating away. Experienced enginemen would deliberately hang back so that they did not suffer a check and could gradually accelerate up to Brentwood. The Class 37s, they asserted, were not comfortable timekeepers on the Norwich expresses.

Another complaint voiced was that the steps up to the cab from rail level were very steep and awkward to negotiate. Train crews were used to them but once a Norwich man invited a boy up to the cab during a station stop. His mother insisted on going too. It was in mini-skirt days and whilst she managed to climb aboard fairly nimbly, she found serious problems in getting back down again. Her skirt was so tight that she could not bend her knees and her skirt was in grave danger of being ripped asunder. The driver was anxious to get his train under way so hurried arrangements had to be made to lift the unfortunate lady down from her cab visit. Volunteers were clamouring for the opportunity!

About three years ago Charlie was working an evening Freightliner up to Willesden with a single machine. Coming up the bank from Chelmsford his locomotive began to sound rough. By Ingatestone Charlie was beginning to feel concerned so he opened the cab window to have a good listen to the engine. He could hear that it was missing on some cylinders and in his words 'sounded like a motorbike'. By the junction for the Southend line it was only firing on two cylinders and Charlie realised that he was in grave danger of stopping completely and could easily foul the junction with his train. He thought it best to pull up just short of the junction. He walked in the dark for a considerable distance down the track to use the telephone in order to inform the signalman at Shenfield box of his plight. By the time that he reached his locomotive again some time had passed but to his surprise everything sounded fine again. He asked the guard (who sits in the rear cab on Freightliners) to use the telephone and tell the signalman to pull off for Shenfield loop. At least, he thought, this would clear the main line. The locomotive pulled away full of life. After the 21.45 Ipswich-London had passed, Charlie enquired whether he should try and get her to Brentwood Bank summit and then coast down to Stratford. Control did not like this idea at all and after a while a light locomotive came past. Charlie watched backwards as lamps were waved about behind him, a lot of activity and general confusion ensued and then there was a crunch and a shower of sparks. The relieving Class 37 was off the road — somebody had clipped the points the wrong way. What a mess! At this point Charlie was able to persuade control to let him go because he was convinced that if his locomotive did start misbehaving again all he had to do was draw to a halt, sit for a while, and the machine would right itself like last time. He left the chaos behind him with the Class 37 going well on the downgrade from Shenfield. He took the train on, with a pilotman, all the way to Willesden with not a sign of further trouble. Back at Stratford it was found that the fuel filters were partially blocked leading to mild fuel starvation. When the locomotive was working hard — like on the upgrade between Chelmsford and Shenfield — there was not enough fuel reaching the cylinders, but coasting downhill the fuel demands were lower and the engine functioned admirably.

Many failures on Class 37s are attributable to the train heating boiler not functioning properly. Most of these failures are because of bad maintenance. Once going, the boilers are fine — the trouble is often encountered in starting them up. Sometimes the secondman has to clamber underneath to clean them out; a very unofficial practice. George recalled the days when it was common to have to stop midway through a run to replenish the boiler water tanks. This often took place at stations where facilities then existed to replenish steam locomotives. A Class 37 holds 800gal of boiler water and it would use 600gal on the outward run from Liverpool Street to Norwich. It was commonplace to have to pull up at Diss or Stowmarket on the return journey to fill up. This was no easy matter, manhandling the heavy leather pipe from the water column into the small hole on the side of a Class 37 used for water replenishment. With cold hands in rough weather it was doubly difficult and both drivers had received many a drenching trying to accomplish this task.

Class 37s also use water for engine cooling purposes and they have produced problems in this area for years. Witness the grilleing which has been removed from the radiator shutters visible on the large bodyside air intakes of Eastern and Scottish Region machines. This has been an attempt to improve air flow over the radiators. Sometimes temperatures could become high enough to trigger the fire alarm bell and cause consternation among the driving crew. One day, George had overheating problems on a London-Norwich run and asked the secondman to give the 30gal radiator header tank a good pump up. This is situated just inside the engine compartment door. George was astonished because after several minutes of vigorous pumping the engine was not cooling down. At the next stop he went into the engine compartment to investigate. Imagine his surprise when he found the second man, sweating away, pumping up the urinal header tank!

Talking of urinals, Charlie related the story of the time when a certain high class driver, just transferred to Ipswich, wanted to know where the lavatory was situated in a Class 37. He went on to explain that he had found the urinal alright, but this was not much use when really caught short. 'Oh', was the laconic reply, 'we don't do it that way in East Anglia, we just do it on a piece of paper and throw it on the fan'. He was suitably admonished!

Whilst Ipswich men have their own regular routes, they do in emergencies get off region with the aid of a pilotman. Charlie related how he had, on occasions, taken Class 37s to Norwood Junction. Not to be outdone, George capped this by saying that he had nearly taken one up the West Coast main line to Halewood. He was taking some empty 'Carflats' up to Willesden where his engine was to be relieved by an electric locomotive. There was none available so George said that he was willing to continue if a pilotman could be found. One duly arrived and the signalman pulled off the road, only to quickly change his mind when he found himself being lambasted by Control.

Both men spoke of the variations that can occur on locomotives within the class — just like steam days. Filters become bunged up and other maladies take their effect which alter performance. Sometimes enginemen find one particular Class 37 that is particularly lively and will take on a Class 47 timing. Locomotives from different depots often perform differently — for example Stratford machines are frequently 'low on amps'. The lesson learned from this evening, however, was just how highly enginemen regard Class 37s, despite their shortcomings. 'They will pull anything, anywhere, but at their own pace', said George.

Their undoubted versatility is a major factor in their popularity with train crews. Equally at home thrashing away on the main line with a passenger train or griding away with an enormous slow moving freight they are indeed the enginemen's friend. This power unit is one of the most reliable on BR and locomotive availability is first class. In July 1971, BR was achieving 88% availability from it and was extracting an average of 52,000 miles per year of revenue earning service per machine. It is a sobering thought that at the same time a figure of 40,000 miles per casualty was achieved. This means that on average an individual Class 37 was failing only once every 10 months — figures that in themselves are testament to a hugely successful traction unit.

Right:
No 37.219 is refilled with fuel at Peterborough stabling point on 2 August 1983 after hauling a freight train from Doncaster. The small covered shed on the right allows basic maintenance and servicing to take place with a measure of protection from the elements. *Michael J. Collins*

Maintaining the Fleet

Above:
In early days the English Electric Type 3s had to be maintained alongside steam — hardly an ideal arrangement. In this view an unidentified Type 3 is stabled alongside WD 2-8-0s and a Fairburn 2-6-0 tank engine at Normanton Depot in March 1965. Beyond a brace of Class 25s take a rest between duties. *Les Nixon*

Above left:
More pleasant surroundings for No 37.087 stabled alongside Class 31 No 31.207, taken during an official visit to Doncaster Depot on 19 July 1981. Routine maintenance can take place in such conditions. *Michael J. Collins*

Left:
Basic facilities for maintenance at Llantrisant where No 37.285 was parked alongside a Class 08, No 08.661, on 1 June 1983. Note the neat numerals on the nose identifying the last three digits of the running number, a feature of some South Wales-allocated machines in recent times.
Michael J. Collins

Above:
Major repairs, overhauls and accident damage require a visit to main works at Doncaster or Crewe for attention. It is at the former where No 37.209 was photographed during an official visit. The locomotive is in the strippers shop, an area where locomotives have to pass through on works visits so that parts can be removed for cleaning and repair. *Colin J. Marsden*

Right:
**Class 37 Cab Layout:
1—Straight air brake valve (locomotive); 2—Train brake valve (proportional on locomotive); 3—Windscreen washer button; 4—Independent brake release button; 5—Warning horn valve; 6—Master switch; 7—Power controller; 8—Main reservoir gauge; 9—Vacuum train pipe/chamber gauge; 10—Brake cylinder pressure gauge; 11—Speedometer; 12—Main generator amperes; 13—Driver's side window wiper valve; 14—Engine stopped warning light; 15—Wheelslip warning light; 16—General fault warning light; 17—Drivers' desk indicator light dimmer switch; 18—AWS reset button; 19—AWS sunflower indicator; 20—Nose light (compartment); 21—Cab heat (half power); 22—Cab heat (half power); 23—Sanding button; 24—Engine start button; 25—Engine stop button.**
Colin J. Marsden collection

Top left:
A Norwich–Liverpool Street train passes Colchester on 12 July 1962 in the care of No D6704. Note the wooden-bodied Gresley coach behind the engine and the Metro-Cammell DMU in original livery complete with front end chevrons. A picture full of historical atmosphere.
Colin J. Marsden collection

Bottom left:
A southbound freightliner is hustled up the GER main line at Brantham single handed by No 37.259 on 22 July 1981.
Michael J. Collins

East Anglian Medley

Right, top to bottom:
A whisp of steam signifies that the train heating boiler is operating as No 37.090 passes Soham with the 08.18 Peterborough–Ipswich service on 5 February 1982. This service was diagrammed to be hauled by an ETH-fitted Class 31 when the 1983/84 passenger timetable was introduced. *Michael J. Collins*

Three 'Polybulk' wagons from the grain terminal at Chettisham are brought through Whitemoor East Junction, March, by No 37.020 on 5 January 1983. The nearby diesel depot has been associated with Class 37s for over 20 years.
Michael J. Collins

A locomotive and coaches substitution for an EMU service is taken down the single line chord to the Clacton branch at Hythe, Colchester, by No 37.110. Although this photograph was taken on 7 March 1982, Class 37s were regularly rostered for Clacton expresses in the 1960s.
Michael J. Collins

Left:

During 1983, the 06.52 Cambridge-Ipswich service was booked for a locomotive and coaches formation instead of the more usual DMU. It sometimes produced a Class 37 for those brave, or foolhardy, enough to get up early to photograph it. On 16 July, however it produced a real surprise in the form of No 37.169 instead of the usual more locally-based machine. The event was recorded on film as the ensemble passed the grain storage depot at Newmarket. *Michael J. Collins*

Below left:

The 07.22 Lowestoft-Liverpool Street has been a Class 37 stronghold for years. In this view, the train was caught passing Bentley on 3 June 1982 with No 37.099 in charge. Unfortunately this train will be withdrawn with the inception of the 1984/85 passenger timetable because of rationalisation on the East Suffolk line. *Michael J. Collins*

Below:

On their way to the 'open day' at Crown Point Depot, Norwich, are Class 56 No 56.088 and Class 58, No 58.003. The pair are being hauled by No 37.219 and were recorded as they left Spalding on the Peterborough line. *Chris Milner*

Freightliners

Right:
A brace of Class 37s, Nos 37.070 and 37.103, pass over the Suffolk Stour at Manningtree with the 12.50 Felixstowe RCT-Stratford Freightliner on 17 December 1981. The Felixstowe trains attract huge loads so the extra power obtainable from double Class 37s is appreciated by the operating authorities.
Michael J. Collins

Below right:
A Stratford-Felixstowe Freightliner thunders through Marks Tey on 17 August 1982 in the care of Nos 37.001 and 37.091 working in multiple.
Michael J. Collins

Below:
Container flats are marshalled in more or less permanent sets of five, and one loaded set for attachment to a forward service at March is hustled through Thurston on 3 June 1982.
Michael J. Collins

The East Suffolk

Left, top to bottom:

The 07.22 Lowestoft-Liverpool service makes a smokey exit from Beccles during February 1982.
Michael J. Collins

The 10.52 (Saturdays Only, Summer Dated) Liverpool Street-Lowestoft is heavily loaded with holidaymakers bound for the East Coast resorts. The train is hustled through Bealings in this photograph taken on 18 June 1983. This is yet another East Anglian working which will be axed when the 1984/83 timetable appears.
Micheal J. Collins

The 07.22 Lowestoft-Liverpool Street accelerates away from Darsham with its seven-coach load on 26 June 1982. *Michael J. Collins*

Top right:

A superb shot of No D6717 photographed shortly after entering service in 1961. It is about to leave Lowestoft with a train for Liverpool Street. The steam-style cast metal shed allocation plate, sited underneath the rear running number, is an interesting embellishment. *Stan Creer*

Bottom right:

Freight traffic on the East Suffolk is very sparse, but the nuclear power station at Sizewell generates a little traffic. No 37.219 will convey these two barrier wagons and brake van down the truncated remains of the Aldeburgh branch to Leiston. Here they will be attached to a nuclear flask for transit to Sellafield, Cumbria. The ensemble was captured on film near Wickham Market on 9 June 1980. *G. R. Mortimer*

Branch Lines

Left:
On the single track branch from Oakdale Colliery, South Wales No 37.162 slows for an unprotected minor road crossing near Pontllanfraith on 25 August 1983. The train is destined for East Usk power station, near Newport. *Michael J. Collins*

Goods Traffic

Left:
Complete with brake tender, No D6793, heads a Tyne Yard-Kingmoor (Carlisle) freight on 10 June 1965. In the background can be seen Kingmoor steam depot, with a 'Jubilee' 4-6-0, a 'Clan' Pacific, and other steam power. *Derek Cross*

Below left:
Descending cautiously down the bank at Churchdown, and heading for Gloucester & Severn Tunnel Junction is No 37.184, at the head of a mixed freight on 15 July 1981. *Michael J. Collins*

Top right:
A Toton-Whitemoor (March) special freight powered by No 37.259 is dwarfed by the huge cooling towers of Ratcliffe-on-Soar power station. It was photographed heading south up the Midland main line on a very dull 21 February 1983.
Michael J. Collins

Bottom right:
The daily Doncaster (Belmont Sidings)-Knottingly sand train, approaches Knottingly yard on 7 April 1983 hauled by No 37.046. Delightful vacuum-braked trains such as this can not survive much longer in view of the air-braked modern image currently being portrayed by BR marketing.
Michael J. Collins

Left:
A mixed freight from Haverfordwest to Carmarthen is rolled through the staggered platforms at Clynderwen, West Wales, on 18 August 1981. The locomotive is No 37.186.
Michael J. Collins

Below:
During the early 1980s, the Class 37s have made deep penetrations into northwest England on duties formerly associated with Class 40s. Threading the platforms at Manchester Victoria on the through line is No 37.015, heading east with freight on 10 June 1981. *John C. Hilmer*

Double Heading

Right, top to bottom:

Class 37s have the Blue Star multiple control system and can thus operate with any other locomotive fitted with the same system. It is unusual, however, to see Class 27 No 27.206 working with No 37.159 on 10 August 1982. The pair are recorded passing Greenhill Lower Junction as they head away from the Falkirk area with a Grangemouth-Paisley oil train. Note that the Class 27 has lost the ETH jumper cables previously affixed in connection with the Glasgow-Edinburgh push-pull workings it once operated.
John Chalcraft

The author can testify that Nos 37.134 and 37.233 made an awesome sound as they banked a Metro-Cammell three-car DMU up the 1 in 37¾ of the Lickey Bank south of Birmingham on 26 October 1981. In normal circumstances this Great Malvern-Birmingham New Street service would climb the bank unassisted but a frosty morning led to indifferent track conditions, the slippery rails combining with an ailing DMU to make a solo climb inadvisable. Banking assistance is less frequently required on a modern railway and sights such as this are slowly disappearing.
Michael J. Collins

Steam/diesel combinations were always uncommon, but this view contains another ingredient of rarity because it features the Settle & Carlisle line where Class 37s have never been common. No D6853 assists Class 9F 2-10-0 No 92249 with a stone train at Dent on 27 May 1967. *John Scrace*

Above:
Nos 37164 and 37069 take an eastbound freight made up of BDA bogie wagons through South Bank, Middlesbrough, on 10 May 1983. No doubt these wagons will be loaded with steel at one of the British Steel Corporation plants in the area. *Les Nixon*

Left:
No 37.089 pilots Class 31 No 31.138 on a very well loaded Felixstowe Freightliner at Ipswich Upper Yard on 22 March 1983. Whilst Class 31/37 combinations do appear on these trains, they are far from common.
Michael J. Collins

Top right:
The heavy Lackenby-Corby train of steel coil is frequently rostered for a pair of Class 37s working in multiple. Nos 37.110 and 37.076 approach Tibshelf Sidings, Westhouses on 26 October 1983 with this most taxing duty. The pristine appearance of the leading locomotive is accounted for by the fact that it was specially cleaned some weeks before to take part in the depot 'open day' held at Crown Point, Norwich.
Michael J. Collins

Bottom right:
Class 37 to the rescue! On 4 August 1983 'Peak' No 45.064 failed just south of Cheltenham with a Paignton-York extra. No 37.284 was summoned to assist and was recorded passing Cheltenham, Landsdown. The Class 45 was removed at the station and the Class 37 continued northward.
John A. M. Vaughan

6
Sphere of Operations

The first order placed for English Electric Type 3s was contracted in 1959 for 42 locomotives destined to work on the Eastern Region. The very first of the class, No D6700 (37.119), was delivered from Vulcan Foundry to Doncaster in December 1960. The operating authorities were impressed with it immediately because it had sufficient power to take on many Type 4 duties but lacked the cumbersome and overweight bulk of many of the Type 4 designs. In terms of performance and versatility no Type 2 machine could live with it so it was recognised at once as a useful addition to the ER locomotive fleet.

Subsequent construction of the 309 other class members were more or less continuous until November 1965 when the last machine was delivered. The orders came in 15 batches and were divided between Vulcan Foundry and the Robert Stephenson & Hawthorn's plant at Darlington. Early deliveries were sent to East Anglia where they were put on express passenger duties. It has been documented that on the Norwich expresses they were regarded as being below par compared to the best efforts of the 'Britannia' Pacifics. They were also put to work on the smartly timed services to Clacton before the advent of EMUs on the line. With the commencement of the Summer 1961 timetable they became regular power for the Liverpool Street-Harwich boat trains covering the former 'Britannia' diagrams covering the 'Hook Continental' and the Harwich-Liverpool Central boat trains between Parkeston Quay and Sheffield in both directions. Later they worked this service throughout, but later still the train was cut back to Manchester so that both locomotives and stock could work out and back in one day. The Class 37s thus became familiar sights on both the Woodhead and Hope Valley routes between Sheffield and Manchester until they were replaced by Class 47s in the late 1970s.

On 5 October 1961, the class made a first appearance at Southend Victoria on an empty coaching stock working but the early deliveries were more usually employed on the Cambridge and Kings Lynn route where they have been the mainstay of motive power for years. Competition with the parallel M11 motorway has called for a speeding up of the Cambridge line services and at the time of writing they are being phased out — Class 37 working to Kings Lynn should have ceased with the introduction of the 1983 timetable but stock constraints have seen their survival at least until October 1983. The switchback and curving nature of this route, particularly north of Bishops Stortford, and the comparatively pedestrian timings, made the Class 37s ideal motive power for over 20 years.

During October 1961 the class began to be allocated for

duties on Humberside when Nos D6730-D6732 arrived at Hull (Dairycoates) after acceptance trials. These machines were officially on loan from Thornaby depot pending delivery of the batch allocated to Hull, Nos D6779-D6795, which duly arrived in 1962. These deliveries were the start of another long association because the class are still quite ubiquitous on North and South Humberside where they operate freight diagrams.

At the turn of the year, on 6 January 1962, the GE operating authorities were sufficiently confident of the performance of their new machines to roster one for a lengthy excursion. So it was that No D6706 (37.006) was used throughout on an excursion from Broxbourne to Birmingham (New Street) via the West Coast main line. The service ran from the London area in connection with an FA Cup tie, the visitor being serviced at Bescot. More recently Classs 37s have become fairly familiar on the southern end of the WCML at least, because one is frequently rostered for the regular trip to Wolverton Works from Ilford with GE line EMUs which need works attention. Appearance of WR-allocated types at Wolverton is also fairly frequent nowadays because they work in on stone trains from Westbury.

Later in 1962 the first allocation to the now closed Sheffield (Darnall) took place, with Nos D6742-D6747 being sent there from new in June and July of that year. These six machines were, no doubt, the very first to see regular service on WR territory, because during summer 1962 they took over the York-Bournemouth through train between Sheffield (Victoria) and Banbury. This took them over former Great Central metals and eliminated an engine change at Leicester. It was during autumn 1962 that Nos D6742 and D6743 were sent to the WR for protracted trials. The trials must have been successful because in November 1962 an £8½million order was announced for 100 units destined for the WR — 70 to be built at Vulcan Foundry and 30 at Robert Stephenson & Hawthorn's.

It was on 17 June 1962 that the very first reported appearance of the class at King's Cross was made, with Stratford's No D6729 in the terminus on a down afternoon relief. On 4 August 1962 the class started more regular arrivals at the station when No D6743 arrived with the 07.05 service from Sheffield (Victoria), returning to the steel city on the 15.15 service from King's Cross. Later they became particularly associated at King's Cross at the head of the prestigious 'Master Cutler' service of Pullman vehicles to Sheffield. The class also worked the expresses to Cleethorpes at this time.

By late 1962, penetration by Class 37s on passenger services between Doncaster and Hull was reported to be almost complete with units operating from Dairycoates as well as Darnall depots filling most locomotive diagrams.

The year 1962 was obviously a year of many 'firsts' for Class 37s as they became more numerous and extended their range. It was on 8 September 1962 that No D6748 made the first arrival of the class at Marylebone. It appeared at the head of a special run by the operating authorities to cover cancellation of expresses on the GNR main line to King's Cross following a serious freight train collision at Offord.

Later in the same month, on 30 September 1962, No D6739 worked an illumination excursion into Blackpool making the first known appearance of the type at the north-west coast resort. This was the premier trip of many because the class were regularly used on dated holiday trains from Yorkshire for many years.

Towards the end of 1962, Gateshead depot started taking deliveries of machines, from No D6784 onwards. The first arrivals became associated with the dieselisation of freight traffic over the Newcastle-Carlisle line which commenced in mid-November 1962.

On 2 November 1962, No D6754 made a trip on the Doncaster-Scunthorpe line with the dynamometer car and 32 loaded wagons — the first recorded appearance of a class member of this route. An unusual duty for No D6728 on 21 November 1962 was a trip up the Cambridge main line paired with EE Type 4 No D209, an unusual combination indeed.

During January 1963 the Gateshead-allocated machines made their debut at Consett. On 6 January Nos D6784 and D6785 brought in freights from Blaydon. On this heavily graded route the machines excelled, proving capable of working unassisted a double load of ore from South Pelaw to Consett. This weight was the equivalent of 18 loaded 21-ton coal hoppers which were previously deemed to require a Class Q6 0-8-0 steam locomotive front and rear. On 4 January 1963, No D6787 worked a freight through from Newcastle to March — another 'first' for the class but surely the precurser of many such trips which still exist today.

Later in the same month, on 23 January 1962, a further new venture by a Class 37 was seen in the trial of No D6737 (then of Hull Dairycoates) with a brake tender between Crofton Yard, near Wakefield, via the Copy Pit route to Rose Grove, Burnley, hauling a test rake of coal hoppers. Outwards the load was 35 loaded wagons and back the formation was strengthened to further tax the machine. In each direction the journey time was approximately $2\frac{1}{2}$ hours and the trial must have been considered successful because this was the forerunner of many such trips by Class 37s. At the beginning of 1962 the Hull area began to see units of the new Vulcan Foundry batch allocated to Sheffield Darnall (Nos D6796-D6801) on the Manchester Piccadilly-Hull passenger workings, whilst Hull's own stud began to be seen on freight workings over the Wakefield-Goole line.

New ground was again being broken for the class because on Sunday 20 January 1963 the 09.48 York-Manchester Victoria passenger working was worked throughout by No D6783. It returned 'light engine' later the same afternoon. These units had, for some time been working the train as far as Leeds, but they were usually replaced by a Patricroft (Manchester)-allocated steam locomotive.

Perhaps the most famous Class 37 duty of all time occurred on 27 April 1963. The then brand new No D6822 was allocated to haul the prototype 'Deltic' from Vulcan Foundry on its final journey to Neasden prior to being placed as a static exhibit in the Science Museum, South Kensington. As train number 8Z02 the pair made their way down the WCML to be stabled overnight at Rugby before making the final leg of the journey the next day.

On 16 June 1963 the Class 37s saw the end of an era when the up 'East Anglian' from Great Yarmouth to Liverpool Street ran for the last time after many years as a named train. It was hauled from Norwich by No D6707.

No D6814 entered traffic during March 1963 and was the first of the batch allocated to the Western Region. From this time onwards they were sent to South Wales in huge numbers. The only exceptions were a small batch of boilered examples, Nos D6959-D6967, which were initially allocated to Sheffield and then transferred 'en bloc' to Stratford. It was in South Wales that the Class 37s found trains and terrain for which they were ideally suited; battling with enormous trains of coal or steel on indifferent track and awesome gradients, the WR men loved them. They quickly replaced surviving steam engines and were instrumental in ousting the 'Hymek' diesel hydraulics. In South Wales each valley has its railway, one or two collieries and its once or twice daily Class 37 soldiering gamely uphill with empty wagons, only to wait at the pit head for them to be filled. In the evening the 37 will roll squealing downhill to Swansea or Cardiff with the fulls to join the torrent of freight on the South Wales main line. Such work is what they were designed for and the Class 37s revel in it.

Perhaps the pièce de résistance of all the Welsh Class 37 workings, however, was the Llanwern triple-headers instituted in spring 1976. The efficient working of a modern integrated steel plant demands a continuity of supply of the basic raw materials — one of which is iron ore. In South Wales, the docks at Port Talbot were the most convenient point for the reception of the ore and special trains were assembled to transport it — usually in pellet form — to Llanwern. Each train consisted of 27 special ore wagons, having a tare weight of 24 tons each, and carrying a pay load of 76 tons of iron ore. The gross weight of each train is, therefore, 2,700 tons. Selected Class 37s had their couplings specially strengthened for hauling these trains. The distance is roughly 50 miles but whilst there is some slow running negotiating the tortuous and sinuous stretch of line near the loading point these enormous trains have to really run. Their maximum permitted speed is 60mph and great importance is placed on punctual running because a late arrival at Llanwern can prejudice the smooth running of the steel works. The sight and sound of these trains worked by three Class 37s working in multiple was truly awesome — they still run but now, unfortunately in the hands of two Class 56s.

In 1964 four Class 37s supplanted steam on banking duties on the Lickey Incline south of Birmingham. Banking of passenger trains under 465 tons weight was discontinued at the same time. Class 35 'Hymek' diesel hydraulics replaced the Class 37s for a few years and at one time a Class 37 paired with a BR/Sulzer Class 25 was tried. Latterly a pair of Class 37s working in multiple has been the recipe but in recent years traffic requiring banking assistance has declined substantially.

In the mid-1960s the WR was anxious to speed up its train services in the interim period between the demise of Type 4 diesels and the introduction of InterCity 125 sets. A decision was made to try Class 37s operating in pairs on its expresses and locomotives involved were temporarily allowed to exceed their 90mph speed ceiling. In June 1965 Nos D6881 and D6882 set a new record for the Paddington-Plymouth-Bristol-Paddington circular route and for a year or so afterwards a few such workings (mostly Bristol-Paddington) were timetabled. The characteristics of their electrical machines, however, giving maximum power output at slow speeds, told against them because it was wasted on such high speed routes. It has been reported that speeds of 102mph and 104mph were recorded with Class 37s on these duties.

On 3 June 1965 No D6988 was delivered to the WR and a new world record was created for English Electric because this machine contained the company's 2,000th diesel engine supplied to BR. Of these 2,000 engines, 1,209 consisted of the 350hp 6KT shunter type engine, but before it was absorbed by GEC the total of engines supplied to BR by English Electric was to reach 2,412 (excluding spares).

Later in the same year, during November 1965, the last of the class to be ordered, No D6608, was delivered to Doncaster for acceptance trials, making a total of 309 for the class. The locomotive was allocated for service from Swansea Llandore depot during January 1966. It is ironic that before it reached its home depot, one of its sister machines was involved in an accident of sufficient severity to justify withdrawal. No D6983 was in collision with Class 47 No D1671 near Bridgend, Glamorgan, on 17 December 1965. It was put to store, pending a decision on its fate, and was condemned during April 1966. The locomotive was towed to R. S. Hayes's yard, Bridgend for scrapping, this making the total of Class 37s to 308, a situation which appertains today.

Scotland at last received an allocation of Class 37s during 1963 when new locomotive diagrams allowed the release of several locomotives from South Wales. A batch was sent to Polmadie and Haymarket depots but were transferred to Eastfield in 1966. Their particular function was to haul oil trains in the Central Lowlands from Grangemouth and they were employed on all the very heaviest workings in the Forth-Clyde area including the heavy Hunterston iron-ore trains which they usually work in pairs.

Another interesting experiment took place during February 1968 when No D6700 was sent to Scotland by Derby Research Centre after being fitted with push-pull controls. This engine was used between Glasgow and Edinburgh in push-pull mode and attained speeds up to 90mph in the process. The experiment was successful, but the Class 37s were not chosen for mass conversion, this job falling on to BRCW Type 2s (Class 27) until the conversion of today's Class 47/7 Co-Cos.

The late 1960s and early 1970s was a period of comparative stability for Class 37s, with no major changes of allocation policy or workings taking place. At this time they began to see some passenger workings in West Wales covering some diagrams to Pembroke Dock and Milford Haven. They also had isolated passenger forays over the Central Wales line. On 28 July 1969, for example, a Coventry to Tenby mystery excursion was given Nos D6911 and D6933, the latter fitted with the obligatory headlamp for this line.

During October 1973, Class 37s were viewed as possible replacements for Class 31s on Paddington-Worcester-Hereford services with a possibility of being able to accelerate these trains. They were tried on six-coach test trains but the experiment did not proceed. The class did make occasional forays away from its South Wales enclave as far as Paddington. On 22 November 1975, No 37.187 was unusual motive power for the time on the 21.40 Paddington-Carmarthen

parcels service. In more recent years, South Wales-based examples have become more common in London and have been known to make appearances at the Paddington buffer stops at the head of failed InterCity 125 sets and other workings.

During 1975, Class 37s began to make first appearances on freight services in the northwest. They became regularly rostered on a Sunday evening steel train from Scunthorpe to Arpley but also at this time they began to make occasional appearances on coal trains in the area, No 37.219 being noted on 28 April 1975 and No 37.245 on a similar working on 5 May 1975. By 1983 Class 37s were common power in the northwest, performing many of the duties formerly carried out by Class 40s. One has even been noted on the North Wales main line.

Very few major incidents have befallen Class 37s apart from the Bridgend accident mentioned earlier. On 29 January 1975 an error in a shunting operation near Marine Colliery, Cwm, Ebbw Vale, led to a major derailment involving No 37.143. Unfortunately, the ill-fated machine toppled down an embankment and the locomotive remained on its side at the bottom of the embankment for nearly eight months. It was successfully recovered and winched up a specially excavated runway to the line during August 1975. The locomotive was set upright and towed away for works attention, reappearing in traffic some months later.

The Southern Region has never had an allocation of Class 37s but from new the machines have made fairly frequent appearances on the region. They have worked the oil trains from Ripple Lane to Salfords, on the Brighton line, and to Earley, on the Reading-Virginia Water line, for many years. They have also appeared from quite early on at the head of excursion trains to such destinations as Windsor & Eton Riverside and Farnborough. In 1975, however, Class 37s started making deep penetrations into Southern territory whey were booked to make regular trips to Southampton on some of the expanding ranks of Freightliner trains. One of the first to work such a service was No 37.057 which passed Basingstoke on a down Freightliner on 15 August 1975. On 10 May 1977, a most unusual combination was noted at Oxford when No 31.231 towed No 37.123 which had failed on a Southampton-Leeds Freightliner. The Class 37 locomotive itself was most unusual power for such a working.

It was in 1977 that the winds of change began to blow again for Class 37s. Odd workings, on freight, had brought the class to Inverness occasionally, but passenger workings in these parts had been unscheduled events. From 1977, however, increasing appearances began on both passenger and freight turns to the West Highland lines. The class began to be transferred away from some of their old Eastern Region haunts, where boiler-fitted locomotives were not required in large numbers, to new fields of operation in Scotland. In later years Class 37s began to be transferred to Scotland in large numbers and now make appearances in all parts of the country.

An unusual duty fell upon No 37.281 on 15 December 1977 when it was selected to haul the preserved 'Western' class No D1023 *Western Fusilier* on the first stage of its journey to the National Railway Museum, York, via Stroud and Gloucester. Five days earlier, on 10 December, No 37.086 had been the unusual choice of power for the 14.23 Manchester-Swansea forward from Birmingham. Another 'first' was recorded on 25 June 1978, when

No 37.223 was recorded at Pwllheli at the head of a 'Cardigan Bay Express' special organised by the NSPCC. Subsequently a few other members of the class have made visits to the Cambrian lines. On 15 February 1979, a further unusual duty for a Class 37 was recorded when the 09.50 Edinburgh-Plymouth express was worked by No 37.016, following the failure of the rostered locomotive, No 55.009 *Alycidon*.

During early 1980 the class began to make even deeper penetrations into the northwest, being reported at work in the Liverpool area. On 23 February, for example, No 37.003 powered a mineral train from Healey Mills to Edge Hill and during the same month Nos 37.078 and 37.171 were in action on the Warrington-Chester line, working trains to and from Stanlow oil refinery. Mid-1980 saw several units drafted to the West Country in order to replace ageing Class 25s on the Cornish china clay workings. They soon put in some appearances on Cornish passenger workings and on 11 October No 37.201 was noted piloting Class 47 No 47.482 from Lostwithiel with the 10.00 Plymouth-Penzance, after trouble with the train engine.

During October 1980 came more news from Scotland in the form of reports of a regular Class 37 working on the Mallaig extension. The machine powered the 06.00 Glasgow-Mallaig as far as Fort William and then continued with the 12.55 Fort William-Mallaig. Also at this time, penetration into the North of Scotland became almost complete when locomotives began to appear on the Oban line. On 31 October for instance, two examples were in action when No 37.115 double-headed with Class 27 No 27.022 on the 07.58 Oban-Glasgow (Queen Street) and later the same day No 37.081 worked the 12.20 Oban-Glasgow. During winter 1980/81 it was reported that Class 37s were having severe difficulties on the West Highland line. On 28 February 1981, No 37.012 plus nine vehicles had lost one hour by Ardlui. Overheating, apparently induced by excessive wheelslip on frosty rails caused further problems and at Crianlarich the locomotive was exchanged for No 37.014. This machine then had similar problems on the climb to Rannoch Moor.

In 1981, Class 37s began to make even further inroads into northwest territory. In the beginning of November, Buxton began to host an influx of the class replacing the duties of the dwindling ranks of the Class 25s and 40s. The Class 37s also began to supply banking assistance for stone trains at Peak Forest. Manchester began to see a general influx of Class 37s and during November 1981 they began to be noted regularly at Guide Bridge. Their penetration into the northwest was almost complete.

At the time of writing the class members are ranging far and wide. During the 1960s their workings were confined largely to their own enclaves. Their great reliability has changed all that, there is hardly an area of the country yet to record a visit from Class 37. From Penzance in the South to Thurso in the North, from Lowestoft in the East to Pembroke Dock in the West, the sphere of operations for Class 37 is now the whole of mainland Britain.

Cambridge Line

No 37.110 makes an impressive sight as it hammers past Elsenham box with the 08.00 Cambridge-Liverpool Street on 26 March 1983. Competition with the M11 has meant that Class 37s are not fleet enough of foot to be competitive on this line and are gradually being drafted on to other duties after an association approaching 25 years.
Michael J. Collins

Leaving the remodelled Cambridge station area, No 37.047 heads for London with the 14.37 Kings Lynn-Liverpool Street train on 5 February 1983. At least two more Class 37s can be seen in the stabling point on the left, and a further example shunts vans in the distance.
Michael J. Collins

Passing Brimsdown is No 37.047 hauling the 11.52 Cambridge-Liverpool Street on 3 April 1982. The alignment of the line is good in the Lee Valley and Class 37s often reach their maximum permitted speed of 90mph on this stretch.
Michael J. Collins

No 37.038 plods uphill through Hackney Downs at the head of the nine-coach formation making up the 16.35 Liverpool Street-Cambridge on 19 March 1983. This loading will be sufficient to tax the locomotive on the steep gradients and sharp curves beyond Bishops Stortford. *Michael J. Collins*

No 37.054 hurries the 13.35 Kings Lynn-Liverpool Street service past the fine manual signalbox at Northumberland Park on 19 March 1983. As this book was being prepared BR announced its intention to electrify the remainder of the Cambridge main line which will make scenes such as this pass into history.
Michael J. Collins

Off The Beaten Track

Right:
On 5 March 1983 a test train to ascertain clearance prior to a steam special working was taken down to Wapping Wharf, Bristol by No 37.254. A train of condemned stock was used in case of problems, and the working is seen at the extremity of the branch in the Bristol Docks area. The Fairbairn Crane, owned and preserved by Bristol Industrial Museum, adds interest in the background. *John Chalcraft*

Below right:
On a day of heavy and continuous rain No D6876 was unusual power on a limestone train from Shap Sidings to Ravenscraig. The photographer was fortunate enough to be able to record the train near Penrith, despite the bad weather. *Stan Creer*

Below:
While Class 37s are common motive power on freight trains in the northeast, they are not photographed every day at Bishop Aukland. No 37.071 hauls the empties from Woslingham Coal Concentration Depot on 27 May 1980. *Brian Morrison*

The Travels of 37.092

Above:
The odd marker light boxes identify No 37.092 as it passes Moira West Junction on the Coalville-Burton-on-Trent line, with the 11.15 Cliffe Hill-Doncaster Ballast train on 25 October 1983.
Michael J. Collins

Top right:
Once again with the odd end leading, No 37.092 is well off home territory as it passes Gatwick Airport station on 1Z41, the 10.02 Norwich-Hove 'footex' which it worked throughout, on 12 March 1983.
Michael J. Collins

Bottom right:
Off region again, but this time the Birmingham area plays host to No 37.092. On this occasion the locomotive was caught passing Norton Junction, on the Walsall-Lichfield freight only line. It is piloting Class 47 No 47.175 which had failed when operating a Cardiff (Tidal Sidings)-Scunthorpe freight.
John Whitehouse

Cornish Interlude

Top:

No 37.207 *William Cookworthy* assists a DMU on the Par-Newquay shuttle service at St Dennis Junction on 16 July 1983. The 16.45 from Par had to be assisted by the Class 37 because temperatures in the mid-90s had made the DMU temperamental and liable to failure. *Geoff Dowling*

Above:

No 37.270 passes along the picturesque banks of the River Fowey as it leaves Lostwithiel for a trip to Carne Point with a load of china clay on 12 July 1983.
Geoff Dowling

Left:

Dominated by the GW main line viaduct at Liskeard, No 37.135 negotiated a narrow bridge as it came off the Moorswater Branch at Coombe Junction. It was working a Moorswater-Lostwhithiel china clay train on 22 February 1982.
Brian Morrison

On the Southern

Right:
The former station at Ludgershall can be seen in the background of this rare view of green-liveried No D6965 of Stratford which is running round its stock after arriving with a troop special from Brandon (Suffolk) on 28 June 1969. The station here was closed to the public in 1961 but remains open for military traffic. *Geoff Gilham*

Below right:
Salisbury Cathedral dominates the background as Nos 37.224 and 37.204 climb westward out of the city with a Fareham-Westbury empty stone hopper train on 16 April 1981. *Geoff Gilham*

Below:
Not too many photographs are taken at the diminutive Dilton Marsh Halt. Heading for Southern territory on 13 May 1981, No 37.220 was recorded climbing towards Upton Scudamore and Warminster with the 03.20 Carlisle-Eastleigh freight. *John A. Vaughan*

Bottom:
Coming off the freight only line to Eastleigh, Nos 37.236 and 37.282 join the Salisbury-Southampton line at Romsey with the returning empty Botley-Westbury stone hoppers on 19 March 1983. *John A. M. Vaughan*

South Wales

Left:
**A fine view of No 37.178
leaving Garw Colliery sidings
with a train of coal for
Ogmore Washery on 15 April
1982. Battling against
indifferent track and vicious
gradients are everyday jobs
for the South Wales examples
of the class.** *Paul D. Shannon*

Above right:
**Passing Class 56 No 56.043
stabled at Canton Depot is
No 37.220 heading west from
Cardiff with a long rake of
vacuum-fitted coal hoppers
on 1 June 1983.**
Michael J. Collins

Below right:
**The jigsaw of conveyor belts
forming the modern Oakdale
Colliery is an impressive
backdrop to No 37.162 ready
to take a loaded coal train to
East Usk Power Station on
25 August 1983. The driver
and second man take a well
earned break before
proceeding, but their seating
arrangements are novel to say
the least!** *Michael J. Collins*

Below:
**Cautiously descending the
Ebbw Valley near Risca on a
hot, hazy 25 August 1983 is
No 37.299 heading a lengthy
coal train. This particular
locomotive was once based in
Cornwall and should have
received the name *William
Cookworthy*. The naming
ceremony, however, was
postponed and this
locomotive was not available
when the new date was set
and another machine was
substituted.** *Michael J. Collins*

Left, top to bottom:

Descending the steeply graded Dowlais Branch from Cwmbargoed Colliery are Nos 37.298 and 37.305 at the head of an MGR train for Aberthaw power station on 25 August 1983. *Michael J. Collins*

A very mixed freight, consisting of an OCA wagon, some CCE department vehicles, and MDO wagons, slowly passes Pontypridd station on 2 June 1983. The locomotive is No 37.230. *Michael J. Collins*

Some fine ex-GWR semaphore signals still exist at Radyr and one is visible in this photograph of No 37.293 approaching the station with full vacuum hoppers from Nant Garw during June 1983. *Michael J. Collins*

Right, top to bottom:

Waiting for the run down to Park Junction, Newport is No 37.189 at Deep Navigation Colliery, Nelson on 25 August 1983. *Michael J. Collins*

This MGR train needed the combined output of 3,500bhp developed by two Class 37s. At Taff Merthyr Colliery, Nos 37.224 and 37.308 creep forward towards the automatic loader of this modernised pit on 25 August 1983. *Michael J. Collins*

With a cacophony of sound one of the Llanwern-Port Talbot triple-headers thunders through Newport on 11 September 1978. Nos 37.241, 37.303 and 37.300 head the train whilst No 37.187 stands in the platform heading the 17.05 to Swansea on 11 September 1978. *Geoff Dowling*

Earth and Stones

Above:
A busy scene at Elderslie — Nos 37.018 and 37.133 passing with a Hunterston-Ravenscraig iron ore train on 19 April 1982. In the background, Class 27/2 No 27.205 shunts a train load of new Ford vehicles being delivered to the Elderslie distribution depot, while in the foreground a Class 26 waits at the signal.
Tom Noble

Above left:
Two green-liveried Class 37s, Nos 6997 and 6943, capture the attention of the train-spotting fraternity as they pass Bristol Bath Road in October 1970. The train is a fly-ash working from Aberthaw power station, South Wales. Disposal of this waste product is always a problem and this load is destined to form infill for the M4 motorway then being constructed. The fine arch of Bristol Temple Meads station makes an impressive backdrop. *Stan Creer*

Below left:
A long train of empty stone hoppers from Westbury to Whattley Quarry hauled by Nos 37.205 and 37.052 prepare to join the main West of England line on 24 June 1983. The lines curving away to the right form the Westbury cut-off, built by the GWR to allow expresses to avoid the town.
Michael J. Collins

Right:

A cold, frosty morning finds Nos 37.159 and 37.228 slowly propelling their train of stone hoppers over the automatic discharge facility at the Foster Yeoman stone terminal, Botley on 3 December 1983. *Michael J. Collins*

Below right:

The 10.25 departure from Marks Tey Yard, Essex is a sand train usually destined for Mile End, East London. Sometimes, however, the train is extended to serve Acton Yard, and this was the case on 17 August 1982 when No 37.049 was seen about to leave. *Michael J. Collins*

Below:

Stone empties from Hope Street arrive at Peak Forest in the care of Nos 37.197 and 37.208 on 18 August 1983. This train, previously handled by double-headed Class 40s, has only recently been handed over to Class 37 traction. *Michael J. Collins*

Left:
This striking photograph had to be included because it epitomises the hard work that Class 37s have been put to in the northwest. Thundering through the sheer sides of Peakdale Cutting with an immense tonnage of crushed limestone are Nos 37.219 and 37.238, recorded on 5 September 1983.
Geoff Dowling

Right:
These interesting vehicles convey lime from Tunstead to Margam, South Wales. The returning empties were photographed leaving Washwood Heath, Birmingham on 8 April 1981 in the care of No 37.086.
Les Nixon

Cement Traffic

Below:
Eastgate, on the Weardale Branch, sees a fairly regular Class 37 working, though few photographers bother to record it. No 37.172 leaves with a full cement train for Thornaby on 12 March 1982.
Les Nixon

Right:
Green-liveried No D6838 leaves the terminal at Grangemouth with a cement train for Northfleet, Kent, on 7 September 1971. This machine was one of a number of Class 37s which were transferred to work in Scotland following train rationalisation in South Wales, which released a number of locomotives.
Derek Cross

Below:
Passing Darlington Shed is No 37.079 with the 17.31 (Tuesdays Only) Irvine-Eastgate cement train. On the left, No 31.121 stands at the head of a Tees Yard-Shildon Wagon Works train on 19 May 1982.
Colin J. Marsden

7
Class 37s in Service

by Michael Oakley

The first route with which the Class 37s will always be associated is the East Anglian main line to which the initial batch was sent. Although one of the few successful candidates for further electrification, the 'Tram Line' has long been treated as a poor relation of the East Coast main line from King's Cross, and it was no surprise that it got second place in initial diesel allocations. A few Class 40s were at first split between the two, but soon they were concentrated on the ECML where they were rated the equal of the Gresley Class 8 Pacifics (which they were not). The Tram Line by comparison received Class 31s which were rated the equal of steam Class 5 4-6-0s, and Class 37s rated the equal of Class 7 'Britannia' Pacifics (which in both cases they were). Speed limits were then mostly in the 60-80mph range, so that for the fastest express work, where steam would in theory have the advantage, there was indeed little in it. For several years the Class 37s successfully worked to 'Britannia' timings between Liverpool Street and Norwich, which seems to have been some people's idea of progress.

Ironically, it was not until they had been displaced by Class 47s to Norwich and express electric multiple-units to Clacton that the Class 37s had the chance to show what they really could do at high speed. Limits have been generally raised to 90-100mph, and when occasionally a Class 37 is still required to substitute for the booked power on a Norwich express, the better examples can still manage the current schedule and load. This is better seen in the up direction than the down, where the incidence of gradients and speed restrictions gives a better chance to assess the power output accurately on this undulating road. Indeed, with the unusual luxury of a completely clear road, except for a concluding signal stop, there was shown to be about six minutes to spare.

Even so, in **Log 1** the limitations of the Class 37 are clearly apparent in the slow accelerations against the grade — speed getting up into the 80s by Diss only with the assistance of bits of sharp downhill, while the long varying climbs to Ingrave summit pulled progress down to 61mph. This is confirmed by the calculated power outputs, which are difficult to estimate on gradients of such short duration, but which show the way in which more than half the nominal power output at the drawbar is absorbed by locomotive resistance at the highest speeds. It is fortunate that the lower rolling resistance of modern BR stock makes possible speeds like the 90mph or so on the gentle descent past Claydon even with power thus restricted. The 93mph maximum rapidly attained near Stowmarket was on a much more favourable downgrade of 1 in 131.

Class 37 use on express work lasted considerably longer on the other Great Eastern main line, to Kings Lynn, where the long speed-restricted stretches across the flattest parts of the Fens offered little scope for improvement by other types anyway. In this case the route is one which seems to get more than its share of running delays, particularly at the level crossings in the Lee Valley. This spoils many a run which would otherwise makes its best speed on this, the best aligned part of the route for the purpose. **Log 2** shows one of the best examples on record of what can be done. This was actually the last booked Class 37 working — though the usual number of substitutions has continued subsequently. No 37.052 was specially cleaned for the occasion, rewarded with a significant turn out of enthusiasts for the run, only for a freight train derailment a few days earlier to require a speed restriction in the middle of the racing stretch at Waltham Cross. The train had to be driven significantly harder than is usually the case to keep time, and the eventual maximum was 85mph.

This is another route with constant changes in gradient between London and Cambridge, but instead of the undulations of the Colchester line there is a distinct rise which steepens sharply to twin summits at Elsenham and Audley End. This typically keeps speed down to the middle-60s, except on the easier climb from Tottenham to Broxbourne where the middle-70s can often be reached. The main interest in the journey was, therefore, in the skill or otherwise of the driving, in tackling the succession of severely restricted junctions out to Clapton, and some of the more awkward curves such as that at Bishops Stortford. In the last few years of Class 37 working the standard Kings Lynn schedule featured non-stop running to and from Cambridge on a best timing of 63 minutes. This was poor stuff by comparison with, say, London to Oxford, reached by High Speed Train in 43min for 63 miles, but this must be seen in the context of the route. To make 'even time' (mile-a-minute average) to Cambridge with a Class 37 is something that is not known ever to have been achieved; the net time of $53\frac{1}{4}$ minutes on this occasion, after allowance for signal and trackwork delays, is believed to be the record for the course. The power outputs calculated may be taken as about typical for the middle speed range.

Coming at the end of the main BR 'modernisation' period dieselisation plans, the Class 37 may be regarded as about the last of the classic mixed-traffic designs; nevertheless, its traction characteristics led to its being recognised mainly as a freight type. This was definitely the case in the peculiar environment of South Wales, where Class 37 power took over the coal traffic virtually to the exclusion of other types.

This was especially a tribute to the capabilities of the design in the Valleys, which feature sustained gradients of a viciousness unparalleled anywhere else on BR, and where low axleloading might have been thought of as a distinct disadvantage. Even with the loaded flow being almost entirely downhill it was a far more difficult task to get the empty wagons back again to, say, Cwm Bargoed colliery on the Dowlais branch, which involves a climb of 1 in 30 or so for several unbroken miles. With the effects of mining subsidence, the true gradients in places could be even steeper than that. Even on the main line, the operating authorities came to have no qualms about running Britain's heaviest train — the iron ore hoppers from Port Talbot Dock to Llanwern — with loads of 3,000 tons including three Class 37s in multiple. This train had to be worked up one particular gradient, the 1 in 93 past Pyle, in the loaded direction. Typically it would be down to about 17mph at this point, which among other problems did not help pathing on a route shared by HSTs which can climb the bank at 90.

Unfortunately there are only negligible performance records of such freight workings, and the reputation of Class 37s in South Wales rests mainly upon their excellent availability figures. When one looks at their handful of passenger workings a more confused picture is revealed. The best-known such workings were the West Wales mail trains

Log 1

Tuesday 8 March, 1977
13.46 Norwich to Liverpool Street
Loco: 37.044
Load: 10 vehicles Mk II stock, 329/340 increasing 350 tons

miles chains		min/ sec	Speeds
0-00	NORWICH	0.00	—
2-30	Trowse Upper Jn	5.30	easy/34 att
5-40	Swainsthorpe	9.12	59
8-41	Flordon	12.14	68/75/68
11-10	Forncett	14.28	70/73/66
14-51	Tivetshall	17.30	69
17-57	Burston	19.59	83/85
20-17	Diss	21.45	83/84
23-67	Mellis	24.29	71/77
28-51	Finningham	28.21	75/73
32-23	Haughley	31.17	85/93
34-48	Stowmarket	32.48	92/89
38-73	Needham Market	35.08	91
42-38	Claydon	37.29	92
47-22	IPSWICH	41.57	—
0-70	Halifax Jn	2.09	38/48
3-59	Milepost 65	5.53	47
5-50	Bentley	7.50	71/80
9-24	Manningtree	10.44	79*/80
11-59	Milepost 57	12.48	64/74
14-59	Parsons Heath box	15.24	72/85
17-11	COLCHESTER	17.44	—
2-48	Milepost 49	4.08	48
4-79	Marks Tey	6.41	65
9-27	Kelvedon	10.29	78
13-00	Witham	13.14	81/73
15-59	Hatfield Peverel	15.22	76/81
19-37	New Hall ground frame	18.14	79
21-70	Chelmsford	20.13	65*
25-48	Milepost 26	23.35	69
28-00	Ingatestone	25.41	67/69
31-32	Shenfield	28.46	65/61
33-32	Brentwood	23.35	74/89
36-51	Harold Wood	32.53	87
39-17	Romford	34.42	81*/85
44-20	Ilford	38.29	68*/75
47-49	Stratford	41.19	54*/59
			sigs 0
51-48	LIVERPOOL STREET =47½	50.50	—

* speed restrictions

Timekeeping: Norwich on time, Liverpool St 3 early
Calculated power output:
1 in 134 rise Manningtree to MP 57: 880edhp at 70.8mph
1 in 178 rise Witham to MP 36¾: 1,000edhp at 76.6mph
1 in 520 fall past Claydon: 760edhp at 92mph sustained

Log 2

Saturday 14 May, 1983
17.30 King's Lynn to Liverpool Street
Loco: 37.052
Load: 8 vehicles Mk II stock, 263/280 tons

miles/ chains		min/ sec	Speeds
0-00	KING'S LYNN	0.00	—
1-49	Harbour Jn	3.24	47/68
6-02	MAGDALEN ROAD	8.15	—
2-40	Stow	3.39	56/64
4-63	DOWNHAM MARKET	6.47	—
3-03	River Ouse bridge	4.18	56/0pws 38
4-47	Hilgay	6.02	62/65
10-07	LITTLEPORT =11½	12.03	—
4-17	Ely North Jn	5.23	62/40*/49
5-52	ELY	7.37	—
0-79	Sutton Branch Jn	3.46	24 max
		4.10	sigs stop
4-65	Stretham Fen	9.18	67
9-26	Waterbeach	13.13	71/74
14-57	CAMBRIDGE =16¾	20.12	—
2-49	Shepreth Branch Jn	4.43	52/pws 22
6-51	Whittlesford	10.09	62
9-77	Great Chesterford	13.11	67
13-77	Audley End	16.57	63*/68
20-08	Elsenham	22.31	65/76
25-26	Bishops Stortford	27.06	47*
28-76	Sawbridgeworth	30.40	73
32-77	Harlow Town	33.38	83
35-41	Roydon	35.40	73*
38-37	Broxbourne	37.57	79/85
42-68	Waltham Cross	41.53	pws 15
45-61	Ponders End	46.27	63/77
49-52	Tottenham Hale	50.02	sigs 26/45
52-56	Hackney Downs	55.11	29*/38/sigs
55-53	LIVERPOOL STREET =53¼	63.56	—

* speed restrictions

Timekeeping: King's Lynn on time, Liverpool St on time
Calculated power output:
Level across Stretham Fen: 1,115edhp at 58.5mph
1 in 150 rise from Great Chesterford: 1,112 at 64.7mph

and their balancing runs, including a trip to Bristol every night to connect with the Paddington/Penzance TPOs. A number of boilered locomotives were allocated for the purpose, basically D6875/D6892, but with mostly light loads and speed-restricted routes, nothing really strenuous was

Log 3

Saturday 1 March, 1975
'The Central Walesman' railtour (part)
Loco: 37.190 Barry to Port Talbot (fail)
     37.180 Port Talbot to Shrewsbury
Load: 10 vehicles Mk I stock, 355/385 tons

miles/ chains		min/ sec	Speeds
0-00	BARRY	0.00	—
0-59	No 1 Tunnel East	3.32	19/13
1-78	No 2 Tunnel East	8.10	17/14
5-11	Aberthaw	13.54	48
9-59	Llantwit Major	24.45	5
15-11	Southerndown Road	40.18	47
19-17	Bridgend	50.21	5*
23-21	Stormy	56.24	50
27-39	Margam Moors Jn	59.50	81
31-29	PORT TALBOT	64-14	—
3-79	Court Sart Jn	7.38	56/29*/12*
6-64	Lon Las Jn	14.03	38/62
11-37	Llangyfelach	20.20	36*/61
15-64	Morlais East Jn	26.31	22*
17-09	Pontarddulais	29.09	42/59
21-73	PANTYFFYNNON	36.10	—
4-39	Derwydd Road	9.30	49
8-00	Llandeilo	16.27	12*/56
12-05	Glanrhyd	22.30	28*/45
15-34	Llanwrda	28.16	4*/46
19-16	Llandovery	34.29	10*
22-46	Milepost 56	40.51	38
23-71	Cynghordy	43.23	29
27-02	Sugar Loaf Tunnel South	51.24	21½
27-59	Sugar Loaf Summit	53.15	27/49
30-45	Llanwrtyd	58.06	20*/54
33-79	Llangamarch	63.07	44*/53
41-06	Builth Road	73.51	5*
43-46	Milepost 35	79.39	30/48
46-53	Llandrindod	83.59	10*/49
53-20	Dolau	94.57	17*/44
56-70	Llanbister Road	100.14	41/58
59-69	Llangynllo	104.06	39/35*
63-58	Knucklas	108.41	51/54
66-23	Knighton	111.54	35*/61
70-42	Buckell	117.16	22*/61
75-79	Broome	124.11	38*/46
78-61	Craven Arms	129.51	12*
83-24	Marsh Brook	137.49	55/51
85-72	Church Stretton	140.46	57/76
92-23	Dorrington	146.28	59*/68
98-29	Coleham	154.49	sigs stop
		155.56	—
98-52	SHREWSBURY	159.07	18 max

* speed restrictions

Calculated power output:
1 in 60 rise MP 56 to Sugar Loaf Tunnel: 1,225edhp at 25.3mph
1 in 74 rise Builth Road to MP 35: 1,320edhp at 25.9mph

required of them. The 1 in 40 start out of Milford Haven, for example, was round such a sharp reverse curve that full power could not be used anyway. Possibly for this reason, the South Wales Class 37s came to have the reputation of erratic performers, and the following two logs have been chosen to typify this.

Apart from the occasional substitution for a Class 47 on a Fishguard boat train, the hardest passenger job for Class 37s in South Wales was the occasional excursion traffic over the Central Wales line to Shrewsbury. The working shown in **Log 3** had visited Barry, and on restarting up the cliffside to Porthceri, it soon became obvious that the usual problem of an awkward Class 37 was afflicting progress. This is basically slipping, but somehow the locomotive can get locked into a cycle of violently running up and running down again about once every two seconds. This transmits itself unmistakably to the train as a series of violent jerks which can go on for several minutes until the upgrade is cleared. The net amount of power transmitted in these circumstances is minimal, which prolongs the agony. In this case it took about 10 minutes of jerking to get up the 1 in 74 to the second Portceri tunnel, with speed fluctuating rapidly and repeatedly down to 13mph. A few miles further on, where the track is nearly level, an even worse attack dropped speed down to walking pace, possibly the slipping syndrome having triggered some worse problems such as a traction motor flashover. Things improved on the main line, where the train was able to run freely with the grade to Margam, but it was thought best not to trust a locomotive having tantrums on the Central Wales line proper, and at Port Talbot it was failed and replaced.

Happily the substitute was on its best behaviour and proceeded to show what a Type 3 can do on mountain grades. These start at Llandovery, where the broad and level river valley which has held the hills apart from the coast suddenly close in to form the coll of Mynydd Eppynt. This forces the railway into a 4½-mile climb at 1 in 50 to its first summit at Sugar Loaf, the easing of the grade by the tunnel mouth standing in the shadow of the distinctive conical mountain from which it takes its name. Progress to the second higher summit at Llangynllo is more broken, a principal pitch being at 1 in 74 away from Builth Road. The first of these may have been taken a little easily in case of slipping, but the second produced a clearly flat-out effort. The specification statistic with which this can be most immediately compared is the continuous rated rail hp of 1,269 at 13.6mph — this is not itself a power specification, rather an indication of how much the locomotive can stand being thrashed at very low speeds, but it does give a convenient rule of thumb for timing purposes, which is that the calculated output at the drawbar should not exceed the quoted continuous rating at the rail at the speed given; in fact it should come significantly below it. At speeds a little higher, it is nothing unusual for the calculated output to come higher, but the extent to which it may do so can be taken as a rough indication of whether the locomotive is a good performer. By comparison with the Norwich run — drawbar horsepower falling to 760 at rated speed maximum — the figure obtained here of 1,320 at 25.9mph is equally a flat-out performance for the type, but it also shows the extent of the 'low geared' tractive effort quite clearly. In a type such as the Class 50, the fall off in drawbar horsepower as speed rose from 25 to 90mph would only be half as much.

Nevertheless substantial variations in performance do

Log 4

Tuesday 26 May, 1981
19.38 Swansea to Cardiff
Loco: 37.188
Load: 10 vehicles Mk I stock, 350/355 tons

miles/ chains		min/ sec	Speeds
0-00	SWANSEA	0.00	—
1-25	Landore Jn	3.09	29/55
4-28	Milepost 211¾	6.53	47/62
7-67	NEATH	11.19	—
2-51	Baglan Bay Jn	3.54	54/68
5-42	PORT TALBOT	7.16	—
3-70	Margam Moors Jn	5.18	65
6-59	Pyle	9.02	pws 20
8-08	Stormy	11.42	37/67
12-12	BRIDGEND =13¼	16.27	—
0-27	Milepost 190¼	1.00	28
3-07	Milepost 187½	4.26	60
5-38	Brynygwynon	6.50	59
6-59	Llanharan	8.11	55
9-10	Llantrisant	10.20	77/87
13-59	Peterston	13.45	68*
17-71	Ely	17.08	76/77
—		—	sigs 0
20-18	CARDIFF CENTRAL =20¼	27.40	—

* speed restrictions

Timekeeping: Swansea 5 late, Cardiff 10 late
Calculated power output:
1 in 93 rise Pyle to Stormy: 1,465edhp at 30.7mph (approximate)
Level MP 190¼ to MP 187½: 1,260edhp at 48.1mph
1 in 157 rise MP 187½ to Brynygwynon: 1,465edhp at 59.7mph

Log 5

Sunday 19 August, 1973
19.00 Skegness to Cambridge (part)
Loco: D6753
Load: 8 vehicles Mk I stock, 266/290 tons

miles/ chains		min/ sec	Speeds
0-00	GRANTHAM	0.00	—
0-37	Milepost 105	1.07	25
3-31	Great Ponton	5.07	54
5-30	Stoke box	7.13	58
8-30	Corby Glen	9.44	83
9-37	Milepost 96	10.30	85
13-21	Little Bytham	13.00	95
16-64	Essendine	15.19	91/95
20-52	Tallington	17.47	93/94
22-05	Lolham box	18.42	sigs 84
23-47	Helpston	19.46	86/90
25-78	Werrington Jn	21.25	sigs 85/0
29-08	PETERBOROUGH =24¾	27.42	—

Timekeeping: Grantham 10 late, Peterborough 8 late
Calculated power outputs:
1 in 200 rise MP 105 to Great Ponton: 1,300edhp at 43.9mph
1 in 200 rise Great Ponton to Stoke: 1,235edhp at 56.8mph
1 in 178 fall Stoke to Corby Glen: 1,020edhp at 71.5mph
1 in 200 fall MP 96 to Little Bytham: 1,635edhp at 91.2mph

occur, even within locomotives of the same batch, and it happens to be a South Wales example which put out the highest power performance in this survey. This was not one of the regular turns but a curious diagram which was substituted for a DMU working for a few months in 1981 and is shown in **Log 4**. It started from Cardiff at 13.50 and worked to Weston-super-Mare, then to Swansea and then back to Cardiff. Although replacing a three-car DMU only, loads unaccountably rose until this particular run had 10 vehicles in tow. This example proceeded to put out its best effort much further up the speed range, in contrast to the last log. It was of short duration so the calculation is not claimed to be wonderfully accurate, but certainly gives some indication that the locomotive is performing exceptionally on this run. To have an excess performance manifest itself at one end of the speed range and not the other is not unusual, and the figures obtained in this case are just barely outside the normal range of performances which are on record.

The non-Great Eastern parts of the Eastern Region have also benefited from the services of Class 37s, but once again it is mainly as everybody's favourite freight power, and the few boilered examples have had even fewer passenger workings. More usually, it is on the odd holiday train that an invader will appear somewhere unusual and provide a performance worth recording. The East Coast main line in particular has, in recent years, never had a single Class 37 working that could be called regular in the sense of a predictable daily diagram for a period of years. At one time a Newcastle to Lincoln train had one from York; odd workings on King's Cross to Peterborough commuter trains have been known, when Peterborough has been stuck for a locomotive and has had to call to March for assistance; the odd Great Yarmouth holiday train has impinged upon the route with Class 37 power in certain years. But only one train has any claim to regularity, in the sense of having been running for several years unbrokenly; this is a summer Sunday semi-excursion run from Cambridge to Skegness, which has had several years as a Class 37 job, and which features the best-known racing ground of all. This is shown in **Log 5**.

Stoke Bank happily features constant upgrades in both directions, as well as the alignment to run at full power without restriction. The better combination is in the southbound direction (the northbound train often gets engineering diversion via Spalding anyway), which gives five miles of 1 in 200 from the Grantham restart, as well as the long sweeping downgrades on the other side. Another good performer, in the log shown, was D6753 — this time in the more usual 'low geared' mode. The resultant hp figures come out in the proper sequence, slightly exceeding the quoted continuous rating up to about the middle speed range, then tailing away in a perfect curve as acceleration continued to maximum rated speed and beyond. This may be taken as most nearly a definitive Class 37 performance as any in this survey. It also made nonsense of the timings, with a start to stop average speed of 70.5mph.

What an indigenous North Eastern Class 37 can do is best shown by the handful of summer holiday workings originating at Sheffield — actually in the proper Eastern rather than the former North-Eastern Region, but usually using locomotives from over the boundary at Healey Mills. The range of such trains has been cut in recent years, but those which would produce a Class 37 were never many in number anyway. This was not for any failings of the Class 37s, quite the reverse, as they were far too precious for the freight diagrams, and smaller Class 31s had regained most of the passenger workings in the 1980s. In the case of the most popular destination, Scarborough, this was no hardship, as the gradients were of no great severity. The one exception was at Flamborough, where the coast line climbs out of Bridlington for several miles at an unbroken 1 in 93. For this reason trains doing the circuit of both Bridlington and Scarborough are usually arranged for the clockwise direction, which gives an easier climb. One of the few anti-clockwise runs on record, however, saw a single Class 37 take 10

Log 6

Saturday 26 June, 1971
14.15 Blackpool to Sheffield
Loco: D6785
Load: 10 vehicles Mk I stock, 340/350 tons

miles/ chains		min/ sec	Speeds
0-00	BLACKPOOL NORTH	0.00	—
3-14	Poulton-le-Fylde	5.38	46/37*
7-36	Weeton box	11.09	54/58
9-58	Kirkham & Wesham	13.40	47*/58
12-28	Salwick	16.48	sigs 42/63
—		—	sigs 0
17-45	Preston	27.48	12*/38
20-37	Bamber Bridge	34.11	sigs 15
24-18	Milepost 30¾	40.41	38/51
28-50	Blackburn	48.27	sigs 10
31-04	Rishton Tunnel East	52.40	39/61
33-72	Accrington	56.29	17*/34
—		—	sigs 0
37.01	Hapton	65.26	57/60
39-11	Gannow Jn	68.18	28*
41-68	Milepost 23¾	72.49e	40
44-30	Copy Pit box	77.42	28/48
48-60	Hall Royd Jn	84.01	22*
52-53	Hebden Bridge	89.08	59/72
57-48	Sowerby Bridge	93.39	sigs 55/40*
59-79	Elland	97.15	64/71
62-52	Brighouse	99.43	50*/65
66-59	Mirfield	103.56	48*/59
69-20	Thornhill	107.10	pws 27/47
72-42	Horbury	111.54	40*/47
76-08	Wakefield Kirkgate	119.43	sigs 0
		120.01	—
79-07	Hare Park Jn	129.43	38/pws 22
81-48	Fitzwilliam	135.19	48/64
85-00	South Kirkby box	139.32	sigs 15/34
85-62	Moorthorpe	141.04	26*
88-35	Milepost 14	144.49	47/57
91-10	BOLTON-ON-DEARNE =127	148.43	—
2-18	Swinton	4.19	44/18*/57
7-25	ROTHERHAM	11.21	—
2-47	Brightside	4.32	50/54
—		—	sigs 0
5-36	SHEFFIELD =8	31.39	—

* speed restrictions   e estimated

Timekeeping: Blackpool 1 late, Bolton-on-Dearne 10 early,
Sheffield 6 late
Calculated power outputs:
1 in 100 rise Bamber Bridge to MP 30¾: 1,200edhp at 34.6mph
1 in 68 rise MP 23¾ to Holme Tunnel: 1,185edhp at 32.3mph

coaches up the bank with speeds in the middle-30s and no difficulty at all.

The one working which did give the 31s some trouble, so that in 1983 it had reverted to the last regular Class 37 working that Sheffield could offer, was the Blackpool train. Blackpool has long been almost as popular a destination for the Yorkshire holiday traffic as Scarborough itself, and summer Saturdays formerly boasted two through trains, one via Bolton-on-Dearne, and one via Barnsley. Local crews were kept trained on the whole route, which at first turned up the gentle climb of the Calder Valley past Hebden Bridge, but then had to tackle its principal obstacle, the Copy Pit bank. This short branch is mainly a freight link, between the Calder Valley and the towns of Lancashire. As such it was built with a twisting alignment and gradients as steep as 1 in 65, as it negotiates the gable between the Yorkshire moors and the open hilltops surrounding Burnley. In what is otherwise a tortuous route with slow schedules, there result pockets of hard work, and on a wet rail it can be as hard a train to work as any.

The difficulties are best seen coming back, and **Log 6** features one of the 10 coach trains that were formerly run. There is no chance of doing much on the level leaving Blackpool, due to the junction restrictions and the general congestion of a summer Saturday. The first real test came after negotiating the former direct route out of Preston to Bamber Bridge, now closed, from where a sharp climb at 1 in 100 gets the line well up the hillside by Blackburn. Copy Pit itself is mainly 1 in 68 in this direction, and at this stage it was difficult to assess power output due to the poor state of the mileposts. In 1974 a completely new set was provided from zero near Preston instead of at Liverpool, and the passing time given is an estimated one for where one of the new posts coincides better with the bottom of the main climb.

Down the other side, the Calder Valley proper runs through Brighouse to Wakefield and has the best alignment of any of the Trans-Pennine routes. Although now nominally closed to passengers, it remains well maintained for the freight and is the best chance for speeds in the 70s. Lastly the vagaries of Summer Saturday operating made themselves felt again, and in spite of being 10 minutes up at Bolton-on-Dearne, Sheffield signal panel stopped the train outside the station for 20 minutes solid and ensured a late arrival. By 1983 the single train was running with load seven only, with every likelihood that the Copy Pit section would be closed completely at the end of the summer season, but the operation of the Sheffield/Blackpool service remains a notable part of the Class 37 story.

And all the time there was Scotland, waiting for its turn. There had been a handful of Class 37s in the Lowlands from quite early on, but they tended to be far too valuable for the heavy oil trains around Glasgow for them to see any passenger use. Emergency substitutions were of such infrequency that few ever got into record; about the only one which ever occurred any number of times was the Glasgow/Edinburgh push-pull services introduced in 1971. Nominally this was the preserve of Class 27s specially converted for running in pairs at either end of six-coach trains. Multiple working was achieved through the normal circuit by fitting the coaches with suitable jumper cables, but they were also modified in respect of fire precautions and other equipment for safe operation of the remote locomotive. Unmodified locomotives could be used, so long as they had standard multiple control system, but this was frowned upon and happened only

Log 7
Sunday 3 July, 1983
15.30 Oban to Edinburgh
Loco: 37.081 *Loch Long*
Load: 7 vehicles Mk II and Mk III stock, 227/240 tons plus ETH
vehicle ADB 97250 *Ethel I* estimated 70 tons

miles chains		min/ sec	Speeds
0-00	OBAN	0.00	—
3-06	Glencruitten box	9.05	22/20/44
6-11	Connel Ferry	15.04	pws 18
8-71	Ach-na-Cloich	19.57	44
12-70	Taynuilt	30.15	sigs 0
17-24	Awe Crossing	38.43	38/46
21-77	Loch Awe	46.13	35/40
24-48	Dalmally	51.05	20*/28
29-24	Milepost 42¼	62.04	slip 23/37
31-34	Glenlochy	66.04	slip 32/39
36-54	Tyndrum Lower	74.35	31*/48
41-74	Crianlarich	83.33	13*
43-39	Pulpit Rock	86.47	38
47-64	Glen Falloch	95.36	24*/46
50-50	Ardlui	100.37	photo stop
		102.34	—
54-75	Inveruglas	111.08	38/46
58-50	Arrochar	117.12	23*/34
62-78	Glen Douglas	127.55	22½/20*
63-32	Glen Douglas summit	129.09	21/46
69-21	Garelochhead	138.45	23*
72-75	Faslane Jn	144.33	40/44
76-09	Helensburgh Upper	149.39	24*/37
78-17	Craigendoran Jn	153.51	18*
81-43	Cardross	158.06	58
85-04	Dumbarton Central	162.45	30*/55
90-02	Kilpatrick	168.57	52/56
91-26	Dalmuir	170.27	sigs 50/57
95.05	Westerton	175.18	extra stop
		175.31	—
96-44	Maryhill	178.55	40/44
99-15	Cowlairs South Jn	184.12	crew stop
		186.42	—
99-76	Sighthill Jn	189.29	28/15*
102-19	Robroyston	194.06	42/63
107-67	Garnqueen North Jn	200.28	38*/60
112-00	CUMBERNAULD =196¼	205.27	—
5-34	Greenhill Lower Jn	6.45	60/52*/58
7-62	Carmuirs West Jn	9.58	sigs 22/44
9-75	FALKIRK GRAHAMSTON =14	14.09	—
2-77	Polmont Jn	5.45	37 att
7-70	Linlithgow	10.35	71/77
12-70	Winchburgh Jn	14.36	74*/78
16-78	Newbridge Jn	17.53	76*
22-13	Saughton Jn	21.36	87
24-22	Haymarket	23.40	39*
25-36	EDINBURGH	26.54	—

* speed restrictions

Timekeeping: Oban 1 late, Edinburgh 6 early
Calculated power outputs:
1 in 50 rise Oban to Glencruitten: 1,060edhp at 20.4mph
1 in 57 rise Arrochar to Glen Douglas: 1,070edhp at 23.3mph
1 in 100 rise Falkirk to Polmont: 1,125edhp at 34.6mph
1 in 960 fall Newbridge to Saughton: 1,185edhp at 82.7mph
Approximate figures due to assumed resistance of ADB 97250

occasionally. The favourite substitution in these cases were Class 25s, and in any case Class 37s (and at least one instance iis known of two working on the job) were rather overpowered for this task.

It was not until the 1980s that an opportunity arose to start the most remarkable series of Class 37 passenger workings yet and **log 7** records one. To understand this it must be borne in mind that the main consideration was not so much power as train heating. The steam boilers generally used on BR had always been expensive and unreliable, while converting diesel-electrics to supply electric train heating was more reliable but even more expensive. As in many things, Scotland found itself at the tail end of the queue, so that when a 'cascade' of ETH-fitted locomotives released boiler-fitted Class 37s from East Anglia and South Wales, it was Scotland to which they went. Indeed, availability of Southern Region Class 33s, undertaking complicated cyclic diagrams from Eastleigh to West Wales and back, released the entire South Wales boilered batch, while steam heat jobs in East Anglia shrank to a handful.

The main immediate use found for the new power was the extraordinary difficult West Highland line. Rumour has it that for years the civil engineers had blocked the use of 12-wheel locomotives for fear of what their bogie wheelbase would do to the lightweight West Highland track. Rumour further has it that, when in time different civil engineers were appointed, they promptly reversed this attitude, in anticipation that the light axleload of the Class 37s would make wear on the track easier. Be that as it may, the long reign of the Sulzer Class 27s came to an abrupt end in 1981 when Class 37s were made available in sufficient numbers to take over completely.

This was not without its difficulties, as the disadvantage of light axleloadings is poor adhesion. It had always been slightly surprising that Class 37s coped so well in the Welsh Valleys in this respect, though it is one thing to keep a slow traditional coal train moving over well-used track with polished rails. It is quite another to go out on the 06.00 train on Monday morning and try the twisting 1 in 58 climb away from the salt spray at Craigendoran and up through the falling leaves on to the hillside at Helensburgh, then on through the clinging mist which greases the rails over Rannoch Moor. Stories came back very quickly of Class 37s receiving a bad name through slipping on the West Highland line, which is grossly unfair, as anyone who knew it could have pointed out — *all* locomotives have trouble with slipping on the West Highland line. The trouble was accentuated, but not caused, by poor sanders, cast-off locomotives with other faults, and the sharp acceleration which was made of the schedules for that time. In fact, in favourable conditions, and once the drivers had become used to them, the Class 37s have tackled the peculiar demands of the job with the same success that they have enjoyed generally.

Train heating, meanwhile, remains a tactical problem. West Highland traffic may be meagre at the best of times, but the high proportion of holiday traffic involved at all times of the year, taking advantage of the growing Scottish ski industry, has for a very long time justified through carriages and sleeping cars every night all year. Traditionally this was an East Coast enterprise, but in the 1970s the working was transferred to Euston. The problem which arose in the 1980s was the scrapping of the ageing BR sleeping car fleet in its entirety and the construction of a new Mk III fleet with electric train heating only. At first it was intended that the

West Highland would soldier on with existing vehicles given a minor overhaul, but loss of sleeping car business on prime routes, as a result of strikes in 1982, caused a rethink whereby all the old cars would be replaced by new ones, the West Highland included. One solution mooted for this was to fit a Class 37 for electric power but this would cause a loss of much needed traction power. The potential was there, and one locomotive was experimentally uprated to the UIC rating of the engine. This was sent to Motherwell depot and it is reported to have been unsuccessful. There were unfounded rumours of mass uprating of Class 37s for the 1990s instead of building new Class 38s. The lack of a medium-powered ETH diesel has certainly come home to roost, either way, and an even more extraordinary solution was adopted in 1983. In anticipation of Mk III sleeper introduction, around October 1983, an initial two Class 25 locomotives which had been withdrawn from service were converted at Aberdeen depot to unpowered ETH vehicles — traction motors and control gear removed, but with engine and generator retained. These were repainted in coaching stock livery and designated Electric Train Heating Ex-Locomotives, complete with nameplates *Ethel I* and *Ethel II*, for West Highland use. A preview of the new arrangements was given during June 1983.

The initial working of *Ethel I* in traffic was reported to be on a Royal Train to Kyle of Lochalsh. Its public debut came as part of an experiment to reintroduce Sunday excursion working on the Oban line, which was included with the West Highland proper in the Class 37 takeover. The stock made available for the purpose was the spare Glasgow/Edinburgh push-pull set, normally used on weekdays between Glasgow and Aberdeen. This was formed nominally of five Mk III coaches, a Mk II min-buffet conversion, and a Mk II driving trailer. It was hauled in both directions on the Oban run, but for the benefit of the air-conditioned stock, *Ethel I* was turned out along with No 37.081 *Loch Long* for the initial working. The run is tabulated on **log 7**.

Nothing much was required in the way of running, which was just as well in view of the presence of the ETH vehicle taking the load well over that which is normal for the route. The train was timed much more easily than is normal for the daily services, with stops for photography at odd locations, and indeed the working was promoted more like an excursion than a timetabled train. The running was more interesting coming back, by which time a damp day had turned to light rain and the gradients faced the train in their worst incidence. The worst of the lot in fact was the immediate start out of Oban, a 30mph restricted semicircular curve up to the rock cutting at Glencruitten, where the disused signalbox still stands, let into the wall of a private house. Wisely this was taken at less than full power. Through the Pass of Brander and along the avalanche run beside Loch Awe the route is violently undulating, but never for more than a few yards at a time; the next real climb is the varying one at around 1 in 50 for five miles out of Dalmelly. Here slight but persistent slipping was immediately apparent. There were no particularly bad attacks such as can occur on Cowlairs Incline out of Glasgow, but again the locomotive was audibly eased many times, and the resultant horsepower figures are very low.

Glen Falloch ('The Vale of Awful Sound'), which name dates from long before the first Class 37 suffered a slipping attack under Pulpit Rock there, is taken downhill in this direction. Out of the woods at Ardlui and Arrochar, however, comes the worst test of the West Highland proper — the ascent of the hillside above Loch Long to the summit niche at Glen Douglas. Here, the locomotive was kept steady as the rain had eased, but again on reduced power. It was not until back on the main line that it was able to show its paces with a much stronger climb away from Falkirk, and in conclusion one of those extraordinary high-speed bursts which a selected few Class 37s seem to keep all to themselves. The resultant curve of calculated power output against speed goes exactly the opposite way to normal, and requires to be taken very carefully in the context of the conditions.

One further question remains unanswered at the time of writing. Class 37 introduction in 1981 was accompanied by a raising of the line speed from 40 to 50mph between the Horseshoe Curve near Bridge of Orchy and Fort William. The section to the south is too incessantly curving to follow this example, but the crossing of the desolate Rannoch Moor and the descent of Glen Spean to Lochaber generally contrive to produce a better alignment. The raise in line speed applied to single locomotives only, however, and did not apply to double-headed trains. Persistent problems with the 06.00 down train on the greasy rails on Mondays have only been resolved by providing a spare Class 20 as a second locomotive — this is coupled inside the Class 37, and at least two examples have been provided with through steampipes to allow heating of the carriages. *Ethel I* was likewise marshalled next to the locomotive on the first Oban run in both directions. Whether the 50mph rule will be just ignored or specially rescinded remains to be seen.

Meanwhile the Class 37 invasion of Scotland has reached its logical extremity, with the drafting of several examples to cover the superlative Far North line. This has been Britain's toughest locomotive assignment for years already, with the work that was extracted from the amazing Inverness Class 26s being a source of unending fascination to those few performance recorders who were in on the secret. It is a measure of the Class 37's success that, in spite of the inevitable number of poor runners received amongst everybody else's cast-offs, it has become even more fascinating. This is more a matter of BR blame than BR credit, ironically, because of a foul-up in schedule. The authorities worked out an unexceptional set of running times, and then booked every station stop for a duration of seconds when most of the principal ones needed five minutes. The resultant shambles has hardly seen a train on time for 18 months, while the locomotive performance has taken on a quality unlike anything seen regularly on BR. The trains have to be driven flat-out from one end of the line to the other.

Nor is this just any old line, like the gently rambling cross-country routes of East Anglia and West Wales, or the enforced grind of the West Highland. The legacy of the Duke of Sutherland has in parts the best alignment of anything in the Highlands, to which only a detailed description could do justice. For, along with all its other extremes, the subtle variations in scenery provide an unequalled setting for the experience. The accompanying **log 8** describes the lightly loaded midday service — the eight-vehicle early down train is normally the heaviest, but also has an easier timing — but a little item like that makes no difference to Far North running. A punctual start was made, gently over the Caledonian Canal swingbridge at Clachnaharry, and then a series of spurts between the level crossing and passing loop restrictions by the side of the Beauly Firth. Not until leaving Dingwall could the train really be allowed to let fly, as the line takes it across the fields and around in a great sweep towards

Log 8

Tuesday 12 July, 1983
11.40 Inverness to Thurso
Loco: 37.261
Load to Georgemas: 5 vehicles Mk I stock, 168/180 tons
    from Georgemas: 3 vehicles Mk I stock, 99/102 tons

miles/chains		min/sec	Speeds
0-00	INVERNESS	0.00	—
1-46	Clachnaharry box	4.23	43/5*/54
3-51	Bunchrew	8.18	11*/60
5-66	Lentran	11.41	20*/67
10-04	Beauly	16.27	54*/63
12-17	Milepost 12¼	18.35	62
13-00	MUIR OF ORD	20.10	—
3-18	Conon	4.09	67/37*/58
5-56	DINGWALL	7.51	—
1-61	Milepost 20½	3.06	49/69
4-14	Foulis	5.30	67/73
6-21	Evanton	7.16	72/75
9-70	ALNESS	11.01	—
1-51	Milepost 30¼	2.20	64/sigs 0
2-68	INVERGORDON =4¼	10.46	—
3-39	Delny	4.59	67/27*
5-22	Kildary	7.19	59/78
7-66	Nigg	9.26	76
9-19	FEARN	11.10	—
2-24	Milepost 43	3.20	69
3-51	TAIN	5.12	—
2-40	Meikle Ferry	3.25	68/77/75
5-27	Edderton	5.42	76/81
7-13	Milepost 51½	7.05	77/83/62*
10-53	Milepost 55	10.08	68/59*/64
13-45	ARDGAY	13.40	—
2-48	Milepost 60½	3.39	67
3-07	CULRAIN	4.39	—
0-35	INVERSHIN	1.17	33 max
2-66	Milepost 64¼	4.45	44 att/63
5-42	LAIRG	8.16	—
2-35	Lairg Summit	4.18	43½ att
5-65	Acheilidh Crossing	7.16	83
9-78	Rogart	11.37	sigs 15
13-03	Milepost 80	15.17	74
13-77	The Mound	16.07	50*/56
15-47	Kirkton Crossing	18.08	34*/58
17-36	GOLSPIE	20.48	—
1-68	Dunrobin	3.36	37½ att
3-07	Milepost 87½	4.53	75
6-17	BRORA	9.45	—
5-18	Loth	6.20	61/53*/62
10-69	HELMSDALE	13.07	—
2-64	Salzcraggie	4.16	56/59
10-47	KILDONAN	12.27	—
2-14	Milepost 113¼	3.48	44/42
3-69	Borrobol	5.48	55/57
7-16	KINBRACE	10.02	—
2-02	Bannock Burn bridge	3.09	54*
3-78	Milepost 122¼	5.18	57 att/64
7-46	FORSINARD	9.23	—
0-60	Halladale River bridge	1.33	52
2-32	Milepost 128¼	3.39	43/52
3-72	County March summit	5.32	50/59
8-07	Altnabreac	10.04	42*
11-52	Milepost 137½	13.53	66
17-14	Scotscalder	20.12	42*/56
19-73	Halkirk	24.07	12*/54/sigs
21-31	GEORGEMAS JN =26¾	27.18	—
0-73	Hoy	1.44	49/30*/63
3-56	River Thurso bridge	4.44	pws 24/47
6-52	THURSO =9½	10.15	—

* speed restrictions

Timekeeping: Inverness on time, Brora 3 late, Thurso on time
Calculated power outputs:
1 in 100 rise MP 19½ to MP 20½: 1,225edhp at 47.4mph
1 in 72 rise Invershin to MP 64¼: 1,255edhp at 37.1mph
1 in 70 rise Lairg to Lairg Summit: 1,280edhp at 36.0mph
1 in 60 rise Golspie to Dunrobin: 1,275edhp at 32.3mph
1 in 60 rise MP 112¼ to MP 113¼: 1,255 edhp at 42.9mph
1 in 60 rise Halladale Bridge to MP 128¼: 1,195edhp at 47.1mph

the beckoning rise which flanks it. A signal stop outside Invergordon for a shunt movement was the sign for any pretence at normal driving to be abandoned, and the locomotive — one of the better ones from the Wath and then Stratford batch — was given its head completely. Racing along the coastal marshes and across the inlet causeways either side of Elderton we all but made 'even time' on the fastest stretch of all. Then the mountain climbing started — not to any great height, but concentrated in the two-stage ascent away from the Kyle of Sutherland valley at Invershin and twisting up the second wooded hillside to Lairg.

Down the less curving stretch of Strath Fleet we fled, missing the request stop at the foot of the bank at Rogart, and then resuming the charge along the undulating coastal stretch which follows. The nastiest pitch of all, the 1 in 60 restart from Golspie, took us up through the woods to where the Duke's statue guards the lineside at Dunrobin with never an atom of slip, and storming away again through the dip beyond. At the crossing at Brora the drivers changed over, strolling nonchalently round from the one train to the other as if it was all perfectly ordinary, and then the magic flight resumed, streaming along the rock-strewn coast to the start of the cliffs at Helmsdale. Seeking an easier path inland, the line strikes spasmodically upwards into the bare moors of Caithness County March as it plunges among the peat streams; no other signs of life for miles all round except for a few straggling sheep and the distant buzzard wheeling on the horizon. For this is midsummer, and the red deer which come down to the lineside for food in the snows are up in the mountains beyond. Then the broken descent to the level treeless fields of Caithness, a world away from the very different level treeless fields of Cambridge. The conditional freight is not running on this day, so the 11.40 locomotive goes to Thurso to change the branch engine, instead of to

Wick. A third driver takes it on the final spurt down the meandering branch, and between them they register the first precisely on-time arrival that has been noised abroad since the Class 37s arrived.

In the quiet beyond the storm, the calculated power output this time is as consistent as could be wished, with very little variation across the middle speed range, and the whole performance almost precisely on part for the class. The average 1,250 equivalent drawbar horsepower from the six sections tried, at 40mph, may be estimated to correspond to 1,310hp at the rail. The published tractive effort curve for the class gives a corresponding bhp of close to the rated 1,750, so this may be taken as the definitive Class 37 performance for power output. Whether it can be taken as the ultimate, so long as the Far North line is there to run on, remains to be seen.

Right:
Starting the run described in the text, No 37.052 powers the last official Class 37-hauled train to Liverpool Street from King's Lynn on 14 May 1983. A headboard was provided by enthusiasts and the locomotive was specially prepared by Stratford Depot. Their efforts were largely wasted though, because members of the class have visited the east coast town in some numbers since this occasion.
Michael J. Collins

Below:
A Class 37-hauled train that will traverse Stoke Bank is the 09.35 (Saturdays Only, Summer Dated) Great Yarmouth-Leeds express. No doubt this is the first time for years that vacuum brake only fitted No 37.093 has hauled a passenger train because it is one of the Gateshead allocated freight machines. It was making a fine effort when photographed leaving Peterborough on 27 July 1983. *Michael J. Collins*

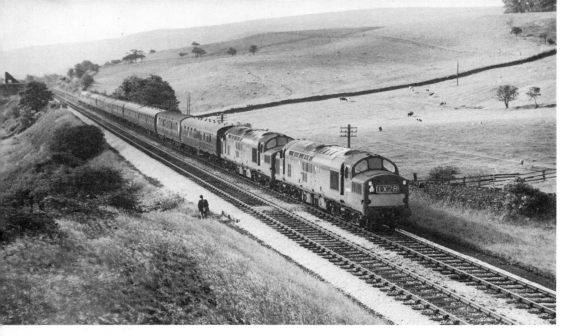

Left:

Green-liveried Nos D6828 and D6830 head down the Copy Pit line near Townley with a Sheffield-Blackpool train on 25 June 1966. *Ian G. Holt*

Below left:

The additional embellishment of a white line just below waist level added interest to No 37.081 *Loch Long* coupled with *ETHEL I* (formerly 25.310). They were heading an Edinburgh-Oban excursion formed of an Edinburgh-Glasgow push-pull set plus a TSOT away from Crianlarich on Sunday 24 July 1983. The 'ETHEL' was included to provide power for the air conditioning and public address systems in the absence of suitable equipment on the locomotive. *Tom Noble*

Bottom left:

No 37.022 coasts the 12.24 Oban-Glasgow Queen Street into Dalmally, one of the crossing points on the single line section. The wet weather, so typical of the Highlands, produces greasy rail conditions which makes demanding work for any diesel locomotive.
Brian Denton

In the Highlands

Right:

A remarkable photograph illustrating how the landscape truly dominates the railway in the Highlands. With Ben Doran towering behind, No 37.108 powers the 07.00 Mallaig-Fort William-Glasgow Queen Street on 12 April 1982. *Les Nixon*

Left:
A charming scene with an unidentified Class 37 pulling the 12.26 Oban–Glasgow away from Crianlarich on 13 April 1982. *Les Nixon*

Below left:
On the Far North line, No 37.017 accelerates away from Muir of Ord with the 11.15 Inverness–Wick/Thurso on 18 June 1982. The sheep seem unimpressed both with the passing of the train and the prospect of appearing in an Ian Allan publication! *Tom Noble*

Bottom left:
A nicely composed shot of No 37.085 arriving at Glenfinnan in indifferent weather with the 12.45 Mallaig–Glasgow Queen Street on 6 June 1982. *John A. Day*

Top right:
No 37.112 waits at Mallaig for the departure of the 12.45 to Glasgow Queen Street on 27 July 1981. The fine bracket signal and the remains of the loading gauge improves the composition and adds a timeless atmosphere. *Paul D. Shannon*

Saturdays Only

Bottom right:
The telephoto lens adds impact to this photograph of No 37.021 hoisting the 09.52 (Summer Saturdays) Liverpool Street–Lowestoft service through Gidea Park on 3 July 1982. *Michael J. Collins*

Above:
Summer Saturdays often give freight machines a run on passenger trains. This was true on 5 June 1982 when No 37.238 of Healey Mills, a machine fitted with vacuum brake only, appeared at Thetford. The train was the 09.12 (Saturdays Only, Summer Dated) Manchester Piccadilly-Great Yarmouth service. *Michael J. Collins*

Left:
The 09.22 (Saturdays Only, Summer Dated) Great Yarmouth-Newcastle train rounds the Ely avoiding loop on 13 August 1983 with No 37.134 in charge. *Michael J. Collins*

Below left:
Approaching the fine bracket signal which guards Mill Green Loop, north of Spalding, is No 37.038 on 4 September 1982. The train is the 08.55 (Saturdays Only, Summer Dated) Newcastle-Great Yarmouth express. *Michael J. Collins*

Oil and Chemicals

Bottom left:
Passing the Midland signalbox at Spondon, north of Derby, on 21 February 1983 is No 37.201, powering the Mondays, Wednesdays and Fridays Only train of chemical tanks fron Spondon Yard to Hull. Judging by the exhaust, the locomotive is trying hard with its lengthy train. *Michael J. Collins*

Right:
A Salfords–Ripple Lane empty aviation fuel train attracts the attention of two elderly ladies as it roars through Finchley Road & Frognall station on 24 July 1980. This North London artery sees a huge flow of oil traffic emanating from the Lower Thames refineries. *Michael J. Collins*

Below right:
Framed in a gap in the fence, a train of repaired oil tanks from Marcroft, near Radstock, was caught traversing the Berks & Hants route between Clink Road Junction and Westbury on a misty 24 August 1983. Traction was being supplied by No 37.294.
Michael J. Collins

Bottom left:
No 37.033 was recorded passing Drumry, one of the western suburbs of Glasgow, with a Mossend-Corpach oil train on 15 June 1983.
Tom Noble

Bottom right:
Although Class 37s are extremely reliable — ER machines currently attaining an availability of around 80% — they do occasionally fail off region. This was the case when No 37.038 expired at Earley (SR) with the 12.45 empty tank train to Ripple Lane. Class 47 No 47.128, was sent to assist and the pair were caught passing Ascot on 8 January 1983.
Michael J. Collins

Scottish Freight

Left, top to bottom:

Threading the River Clyde valley near Abington is green-liveried No D6905 at the head of a down goods. What a difference it has made to this view since 25kV ac electrification has been erected on the West Coast main line. *John Cooper-Smith*

A south bound train of car-flats heads up the ECML at Grantshouse behind No 6728 on 27 June 1970. *Derek Cross*

The neat headlight recently fitted to most Scottish examples of Class 37s is clearly visible on No 37.011, as it passes Burntisland with a short air-braked freight on 14 June 1983. *Steve Turner*

Bottom left:

The novel signalbox at Corrour makes an interesting foreground as No 37.012 arrives with the Mossend-Corpach freight on 28 August 1981. *Kim Fullbrook*

Bottom right:

The uprated No 37.292 leads No 37.145 on a train of empty coal hoppers from Ravenscraig, en route to Hunterston on 5 November 1981. The electric maintenance depot at Shields Road, Glasgow, can be discerned in the right background. *Tom Noble*

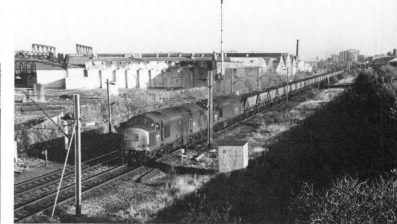

114

Short Trains

Right:
On 2 August 1983, the General Manager visited the Pembroke Dock branch. Leaving Narbeth with the GM Inspection Saloon is an immaculate No 37.302 bound for Pembroke Dock. This locomotive is one of the group fitted with specially strengthened couplings for the Llanwern triple-headed workings, but since Class 37s have been replaced by Class 56s on this diagram they have reverted to normal duties, retaining their strengthened couplings.
John A. M.. Vaughan

Below right:
This interesting train is a single FBB vehicle containing whisky. It is arriving at Millerhill behind No 37.148. The combination of the steam-age water tower and modern electronic signalling in the background is slightly incongruous. *Michael Rhodes*

Below:
The daily (as required) Diss–Ipswich freight consisted of only two vehicles plus a brakevan as it approached Stowmarket behind No 37.172 on 20 August 1982. In the background, a Metro-Cammell three-car DMU forms an Ipswich–Cambridge service.
Michael J. Collins

Semaphores

Left:
A fine array of semaphore signals still exist at Ely Dock Junction though these will shortly be replaced by MAS as the Cambridge area resignalling scheme gains momentum. With part of Ely Cathedral on the left, No 37.109 passes on 13 August 1983 with the 08.32 Norwich-Liverpool Street which runs via Cambridge. *Michael J. Collins*

Right:
Semaphore signals everywhere on 6 April 1983 as No 37.028 passes Goose Hill Junction, Normanton, with a southbound train of bolster wagons. The novel method employed to secure the vestibule doors on this machine is interesting. *Michael J. Collins*

Below left:
On the sultry afternoon on 20 August 1983, No 37.082 passes a bracket signal at Brandon, Suffolk, with the 14.34 (Summer Dated, Saturdays Only) Great Yarmouth-Manchester Piccadilly express. Non-ETH fitted Class 37s cannot survive for much longer hauling trains such as these, because in just a short time steam-heated carriage stock will be a thing of the past. *Michael J. Collins*

Special Traffic

Left, top to bottom:

On 630V dc third-rail territory, an 'Adex' from the Midland Region is powered over the North London Line at Brondesbury by No 37.052 during February 1982.
Michael J. Collins

No 37.090 powered an F&W Railtours' enthusiasts' special over the single-track Wisbech branch on 12 February 1982. Entitled 'The Joint Line Bumper' the train had originated in Plymouth and had traversed the doomed Spalding-March section of the GN/GE joint line.
Michael J. Collins

North Staffordshire Junction, between Burton-on-Trent and Derby, can be seen in the background as No 37.183 passes with 'The Freightliner' railtour on 19 April 1980.
Bert Wynn

Right, top to bottom:

A gem from the past as No D6840 passes Alloway Junction with a Greenock-Heads of Ayr company excursion. An advertisement for ladies underwear seems somewhat misplaced on the front of a Class 37!
Derek Cross

Locomotive-hauled trains are frowned upon when visiting the Central Wales line currently because of the poor state of the track and infrastructure. In happier times the line had a number of visits from Class 37s on special excursions; one such occasion was 22 March 1980 when Nos 37.179 and 37.182 were recorded at Llanwrtyd Wells with the 'Red Dragon' chartex. *A. D. Pullar*

The Spalding Tulip Parade always attracts a number of special trains from far flung parts of the country. Thronged by visitors, No 37.110 prepares to get the 18.35 return excursion to Norwich under way on 8 May 1982. *Michael J. Collins*

Appendices
1 Class 37 Numberings and Locomotive Data

Original Number	TOPS Number	Works Number	EE Number	Date to Traffic	Present Status Brakes	Heat	Twin Tanks	First Allocation
D6700	37.119	VF579	2863	12/60	D	o		Stratford
D6701	37.001	VF580	2864	11/60	D	o		Stratford
D6702	37.002	VF581	2865	11/60	D	o	*	Stratford
D6703	37.003	VF582	2866	12/60	V	o	*	Stratford
D6704	37.004	VF583	2867	12/60	D	o		Stratford
D6705	37.005	VF584	2868	12/60	V	o	*	Stratford
D6706	37.006	VF585	2869	1/61	D	o	*	March
D6707	37.007	VF586	2870	2/61	D	o	*	March
D6708	37.008	VF587	2871	2/61	D	o	*	Ipswich
D6709	37.009	VF588	2872	3/61	D	o	*	Stratford
D6710	37.010	VF589	2873	3/61	D	o		Stratford
D6711	37.011	VF590	2874	3/61	D	b		Stratford
D6712	37.012	VF591	2875	3/61	D	b		Stratford
D6713	37.013	VF592	2876	4/61	V	o		Stratford
D6714	37.014	VF593	2877	4/61	D	b		Stratford
D6715	37.015	VF594	2878	6/61	D	o	*	Stratford
D6716	37.016	VF595	2879	6/61	D	o		Stratford
D6717	37.017	VF596	2880	6/61	V	b		Stratford
D6718	37.018	VF597	2881	6/61	D	o		Stratford
D6719	37.019	VF598	2882	7/61	D	o		Stratford
D6720	37.020	VF599	2883	7/61	D	o	*	Stratford
D6721	37.021	VF600	2884	7/61	D	b		Norwich
D6722	37.022	VF601	2885	7/61	D	b		Norwich
D6723	37.023	VF602	2886	7/61	V	i		March
D6724	37.024	VF603	2887	8/61	D	o		March
D6725	37.025	VF604	2888	8/61	D	b		Stratford
D6726	37.026	VF605	2889	9/61	D	b		Stratford
D6727	37.027	VF606	2890	9/61	D	b		Stratford
D6728	37.028	VF607	2891	10/61	V	o		Stratford
D6729	37.029	VF608	2892	10/61	D	o	*	Stratford
D6730	37.030	VF609	2893	10/61	D	o	*	Dairycoates
D6731	37.031	VF610	2894	11/61	D	o	*	Dairycoates
D6732	37.032	VF611	2895	3/62	D	o	*	Dairycoates
D6733	37.033	VF612	2896	3/62	D	b		Dairycoates
D6734	37.034	VF613	2897	3/62	D	i		Dairycoates
D6735	37.035	VF614	2898	5/62	D	b		Dairycoates
D6736	37.036	VF615	2899	5/62	V	b		Dairycoates
D6737	37.037	VF616	2900	5/62	D	b		Dairycoates
D6738	37.038	VF617	2901	5/62	D	b		Dairycoates
D6739	37.039	VF618	2902	5/62	D	b		Dairycoates
D6740	37.040	VF619	2903	6/62	D	o		Dairycoates
D6741	37.041	VF620	2904	6/62	D	i		Dairycoates

Original Number	TOPS Number	Works Number	EE Number	Date to Traffic	Present Status Brakes	Heat	Twin Tanks	First Allocation
D6742	37.042	VF696	3034	6/62	D	o	*	Darnall
D6743	37.043	VF697	3035	6/62	D	b		Darnall
D6744	37.044	VF698	3036	6/62	D	b		Darnall
D6745	37.045	VF699	3037	7/62	D	o	*	Darnall
D6746	37.046	VF700	3038	7/62	D	o		Darnall
D6747	37.047	VF701	3039	7/62	D	i		Darnall
D6748	37.048	VF702	3040	8/62	D	o		Darnall
D6749	37.049	VF703	3041	8/62	D	b		Darnall
D6750	37.050	VF704	3042	8/62	D	b		Darnall
D6751	37.051	VF705	3043	8/62	D	b		Darnall
D6752	37.052	VF706	3044	9/62	D	b		Darnall
D6753	37.053	VF707	3045	9/62	D	o		Darnall
D6754	37.054	VF708	3046	9/62	D	b		Darnall
D6755	37.055	VF709	3047	9/62	D	o		Thornaby
D6756	37.056	VF710	3048	9/62	D	o		Thornaby
D6757	37.057	VF711	3049	10/62	D	o		Thornaby
D6758	37.058	VF712	3050	10/62	V	o	*	Thornaby
D6759	37.059	VF713	3051	10/62	D	o	*	Thornaby
D6760	37.060	VF714	3052	10/62	D	o		Thornaby
D6761	37.061	VF715	3053	10/62	V	o	*	Thornaby
D6762	37.062	VF716	3054	10/62	V	o	*	Thornaby
D6763	37.063	VF717	3055	11/62	D	o	*	Thornaby
D6764	37.064	VF718	3056	11/62	D	o		Thornaby
D6765	37.065	VF719	3057	11/62	D	o	*	Thornaby
D6766	37.066	VF720	3058	11/62	V	o	*	Thornaby
D6767	37.067	VF721	3059	11/62	D	o	*	Thornaby
D6768	37.068	VF722	3060	11/62	D	o	*	Thornaby
D6769	37.069	RSH8315	3061	7/62	D	o	*	Thornaby
D6770	37.070	RSH8316	3062	8/62	D	o		Thornaby
D6771	37.071	RSH8317	3063	8/62	D	o	*	Thornaby
D6772	37.072	RSH8318	3064	9/62	D	o	*	Thornaby
D6773	37.073	RSH8319	3065	9/62	D	o	*	Thornaby
D6774	37.074	RSH8320	3066	9/62	D	o		Thornaby
D6775	37.075	RSH8321	3067	9/62	V	b		Thornaby
D6776	37.076	RSH8322	3068	10/62	D	o	*	Thornaby
D6777	37.077	RSH8323	3069	10/62	D	o		Thornaby
D6778	37.078	RSH8324	3070	10/62	D	o	*	Thornaby
D6779	37.079	RSH8325	3206	11/62	D	o	*	Dairycoates
D6780	37.080	RSH8326	3207	11/62	D	o		Dairycoates
D6781	37.081	RSH8327	3208	11/62	D	b		Dairycoates
D6782	37.082	RSH8328	3209	11/62	V	o	*	Dairycoates
D6783	37.083	RSH8329	3210	12/62	V	o	*	Dairycoates
D6784	37.084	RSH8330	3211	12/62	D	b		Gateshead
D6785	37.085	RSH8331	3212	12/62	D	b		Gateshead
D6786	37.086	RSH8332	3213	12/62	D	b		Gateshead
D6787	37.087	RSH8333	3214	12/62	D	b		Gateshead
D6788	37.088	RSH8334	3215	1/63	D	b		Gateshead
D6789	37.089	RSH8335	3216	1/63	D	i		Gateshead
D6790	37.090	RSH8336	3217	1/63	V	b		Gateshead
D6791	37.091	RSH8337	3218	1/63	D	b		Gateshead
D6792	37.092	RSH8338	3219	2/63	D	b		Gateshead
D6793	37.093	RSH8339	3220	2/63	V	o	*	Gateshead
D6794	37.094	RSH8341	3221	2/63	D	o		Gateshead
D6795	37.095	RSH8342	3222	3/63	D	o	*	Gateshead
D6796	37.096	VF750	3225	11/62	D	o	*	Darnall
D6797	37.097	VF751	3226	12/62	V	b		Darnall
D6798	37.098	VF752	3227	12/62	D	o	*	Darnall
D6799	37.099	VF753	3228	12/62	D	b		Darnell
D6800	37.100	VF754	3229	12/62	V	o	*	Darnall
D6801	37.101	VF755	3230	12/62	D	o	*	Darnall

Original Number	TOPS Number	Works Number	EE Number	Date to Traffic	Present Status Brakes	Heat	Twin Tanks	First Allocation
D6802	37.102	VF756	3231	1/63	D	b		Darnall
D6803	37.103	VF757	3232	1/63	D	i		Darnall
D6804	37.104	VF758	3233	1/63	D	o		Darnall
D6805	37.105	VF759	3234	1/63	D	o		Darnall
D6806	37.106	VF760	3235	1/63	D	o	*	Darnall
D6807	37.107	VF761	3236	1/63	D	b		Darnall
D6808	37.108	VF762	3237	1/63	D	b		Darnall
D6809	37.109	VF763	3238	2/63	D	b		Darnall
D6810	37.110	VF764	3239	2/63	D	b		Darnall
D6811	37.111	VF765	3240	2/63	D	b		Darnall
D6812	37.112	VF766	3241	2/63	D	b		Darnall
D6813	37.113	VF767	3242	2/63	D	o		Darnall
D6814	37.114	VF768	3243	2/63	D	b		Darnall
D6815	37.115	VF769	3244	2/63	D	b		Darnall
D6816	37.116	VF770	3245	3/63	D	i		Darnall
D6817	37.117	VF771	3246	3/63	D	o	*	Darnall
D6818	37.118	VF772	3247	3/63	D	i		Darnall
D6819	37.283	RSH8379	3264	4/63	D	o		Canton
D6820	37.120	RSH8380	3265	4/63	D	o		Canton
D6821	37.121	RSH8381	3266	4/63	D	o		Canton
D6822	37.122	RSH8382	3267	4/63	D	o		Canton
D6823	37.123	RSH8383	3268	4/63	D	o		Canton
D6824	37.124	RSH8384	3269	5/63	D	o		Canton
D6825	37.125	RSH8385	3270	5/63	D	o		Canton
D6826	37.126	RSH8386	3271	5/63	D	o		Canton
D6827	37.127	RSH8387	3272	5/63	D	o		Canton
D6828	37.128	RSH8388	3273	6/63	D	o		Canton
D6829	37.129	VF803	3274	4/63	D	o		Canton
D6830	37.130	VF804	3275	4/63	D	o		Canton
D6831	37.131	VF805	3276	4/63	D	o		Canton
D6832	37.132	VF806	3277	5/63	D	o		Canton
D6833	37.133	VF807	3278	4/63	D	o		Canton
D6834	37.134	VF808	3279	4/63	D	o		Canton
D6835	37.135	VF809	3280	4/63	D	o		Canton
D6836	37.136	VF810	3281	4/63	D	o		Canton
D6837	37.137	VF811	3282	5/63	D	o		Llandore
D6838	37.138	VF812	3283	5/63	D	o		Canton
D6839	37.139	VF813	3314	5/63	D	o		Canton
D6840	37.140	VF814	3315	5/63	D	o		Canton
D6841	37.141	VF815	3316	5/63	D	o		Canton
D6842	37.142	VF816	3317	5/63	D	o		Canton
D6843	37.143	VF817	3318	5/63	D	o		Canton
D6844	37.144	VF818	3319	6/63	D	o		Canton
D6845	37.145	VF819	3320	6/63	D	o		Canton
D6846	37.146	VF820	3321	6/63	D	o		Canton
D6847	37.147	VF821	3322	6/63	D	o		Canton
D6848	37.148	VF822	3323	6/63	D	o		Canton
D6849	37.149	VF823	3324	6/63	D	o		Canton
D6850	37.150	VF824	3325	6/63	D	o		Canton
D6851	37.151	VF825	3326	6/63	D	o		Canton
D6852	37.152	VF826	3327	7/63	D	o		Llandore
D6853	37.153	VF827	3328	7/63	D	o		Llandore
D6854	37.154	VF828	3329	7/63	D	o		Llandore
D6855	37.155	VF829	3330	7/63	D	o		Llandore
D6856	37.156	VF830	3331	7/63	D	o		Llandore
D6857	37.157	VF831	3332	7/63	D	o		Canton
D6858	37.158	VF832	3333	8/63	D	o		Llandore
D6859	37.159	RSH8390	3337	6/63	D	o		Canton
D6860	37.160	RSH8391	3338	7/63	D	o		Canton
D6861	37.161	RSH8392	3339	7/63	D	o	*	Llandore

Original Number	TOPS Number	Works Number	EE Number	Date to Traffic	Present Status Brakes	Heat	Twin Tanks	First Allocation
D6862	37.162	RSH8393	3340	8/63	D	o	*	Llandore
D6863	37.163	RSH8394	3341	8/63	D	o	*	Llandore
D6864	37.164	RSH8395	3342	8/63	D	o	*	Llandore
D6865	37.165	RSH8396	3343	9/63	D	o	*	Llandore
D6866	37.166	RSH8397	3344	9/63	D	o		Ebbw Junc
D6867	37.167	RSH8398	3345	9/63	D	o	*	Ebbw Junc
D6868	37.168	RSH8399	3346	10/63	D	o		Ebbw Junc
D6869	37.169	VF833	3347	8/63	D	o		Llandore
D6870	37.170	VF834	3348	9/63	D	o		Llandore
D6871	37.171	VF835	3349	9/63	D	o		Canton
D6872	37.172	VF836	3350	9/63	D	o		Ebbw Junc
D6873	37.173	VF837	3351	9/63	D	o		Llandore
D6874	37.174	VF838	3352	9/63	D	o		Ebbw Junc
D6875	37.175	VF839	3353	9/63	D	b		Ebbw Junc
D6876	37.176	VF840	3354	10/63	D	b		Ebbw Junc
D6877	37.177	VF841	3355	10/63	D	b		Ebbw Junc
D6878	37.178	VF842	3356	10/63	D	b		Ebbw Junc
D6879	37.179	RSH8400	3357	10/63	D	i		Ebbw Junc
D6880	37.180	RSH8401	3358	10/63	D	b		Llandore
D6881	37.181	RSH8402	3359	10/63	D	b		Canton
D6882	37.182	RSH8403	3360	10/60	D	b		Canton
D6883	37.183	RSH8404	3361	11/63	D	b		Llandore
D6884	37.184	RSH8405	3362	11/63	D	b		Llandore
D6885	37.185	RSH8406	3363	1/64	D	b		Llandore
D6886	37.186	RSH8407	3364	12/63	D	b		Llandore
D6887	37.187	RSH8408	3365	1/64	D	b		Llandore
D6888	37.188	RSH8409	3366	1/64	D	b		Llandore
D6889	37.189	RSH8410	3367	1/64	D	b		Canton
D6890	37.190	RSH8411	3368	1/64	D	b		Llandore
D6891	37.191	RSH8412	3369	2/64	D	b		Llandore
D6892	37.192	RSH8413	3370	2/64	D	b		Llandore
D6893	37.193	RSH8414	3371	2/64	D	o	*	Llandore
D6894	37.194	RSH8415	3372	3/64	D	o	*	Llandore
D6895	37.195	RSH8416	3373	3/64	D	o	*	Llandore
D6896	37.196	RSH8417	3374	4/64	V	o		Llandore
D6897	37.197	RSH8418	3375	4/64	D	o	*	Llandore
D6898	37.198	RSH8419	3376	4/64	D	o	*	Llandore
D6899	37.199	VF843	3377	10/63	D	o	*	Canton
D6900	37.200	VF844	3378	10/63	D	o	*	Canton
D6901	37.201	VF845	3379	10/63	D	o		Canton
D6902	37.202	VF846	3380	10/63	D	o		Canton
D6903	37.203	VF847	3381	10/63	D	o		Canton
D6904	37.204	VF848	3382	11/63	D	o		Canton
D6905	37.205	VF849	3383	11/63	D	o	*	Llandore
D6906	37.206	VF850	3384	11/63	D	o		Llandore
D6907	37.207	VF851	3385	11/63	D	o		Llandore
D6908	37.208	VF852	3386	11/63	D	o		Llandore
D6909	37.209	VF853	3387	1/64	D	o		Llandore
D6910	37.210	VF854	3388	11/63	D	o	*	Llandore
D6911	37.211	VF855	3389	12/63	D	o		Llandore
D6912	37.212	VF856	3390	1/64	D	o	*	Llandore
D6913	37.213	VF857	3391	1/64	D	o	*	Llandore
D6914	37.214	VF858	3392	1/64	V	o	*	Canton
D6915	37.215	VF859	3393	1/64	D	o		Llandore
D6916	37.216	VF860	3394	1/64	D	o	*	Llandore
D6917	37.217	VF861	3295	1/64	V	o	*	Llandore
D6918	37.218	VF862	3396	1/64	D	o		Llandore
D6919	37.219	VF863	3405	1/64	D	o		Canton
D6920	37.220	VF864	3406	1/64	D	o	*	Canton
D6921	37.221	VF865	3407	1/64	D	o		Llandore

Original Number	TOPS Number	Works Number	EE Number	Date to Traffic	Present Status Brakes	Heat	Twin Tanks	First Allocation
D6922	37.222	VF866	3408	1/64	V	o	*	Llandore
D6923	37.223	VF867	3409	2/64	D	o	*	Llandore
D6924	37.224	VF868	3410	2/64	D	o	*	Llandore
D6925	37.225	VF869	3411	2/64	V	o	*	Llandore
D6926	37.226	VF870	3412	2/64	D	o		Llandore
D6927	37.227	VF871	3413	2/64	D	o	*	Llandore
D6928	37.228	VF872	3414	2/64	V	o	*	Llandore
D6929	37.229	VF873	3415	2/64	V	o	*	Llandore
D6930	37.230	VF874	3416	3/64	V	o	*	Llandore
D6931	37.231	VF875	3417	3/64	D	o	*	Llandore
D6932	37.232	VF876	3418	3/64	D	o		Llandore
D6933	37.233	VF877	3419	4/64	D	o		Llandore
D6934	37.234	VF878	3420	4/64	D	o	*	Llandore
D6935	37.235	VF879	3421	4/64	V	o	*	Llandore
D6936	37.236	VF880	3422	4/64	D	o	*	Llandore
D6937	37.237	VF881	3423	5/64	D	o		Canton
D6938	37.238	VF882	3424	6/64	D	o		Canton
D6939	37.239	VF927	3496	10/64	V	o	*	Canton
D6940	37.240	VF928	3497	10/64	D	o	*	Canton
D6941	37.241	VF929	3498	10/64	D	o		Canton
D6942	37.242	VF930	3499	10/64	D	o	*	Canton
D6943	37.243	VF931	3500	10/64	D	o	*	Canton
D6944	37.244	VF932	3501	10/64	D	o	*	Canton
D6945	37.245	VF933	3502	10/64	D	o		Canton
D6946	37.246	VF934	3503	10/64	D	o		Canton
D6947	37.247	VF935	3504	11/64	D	b		Canton
D6948	37.248	VF936	3505	11/64	D	o	*	Canton
D6949	37.249	VF937	3506	12/64	D	o		Canton
D6950	37.250	VF938	3507	12/64	D	o	*	Canton
D6951	37.251	VF939	3508	1/65	V	o	*	Canton
D6952	37.252	VF940	3509	1/65	D	o		Canton
D6953	37.253	VF941	3510	1/65	V	o		Canton
D6954	37.254	VF942	3511	1/65	D	o	*	Canton
D6955	37.255	VF943	3512	1/65	D	o	*	Canton
D6956	37.256	VF944	3513	1/65	D	o		Canton
D6957	37.257	VF945	3514	1/65	D	o	*	Canton
D6958	37.258	VF946	3515	1/65	D	o	*	Canton
D6959	37.259	VF948	3519	2/65	D	o		Tinsley
D6960	37.260	VF949	3520	2/65	D	b		Tinsley
D6961	37.261	VF950	3521	2/65	D	b		Tinsley
D6962	37.262	VF951	3522	2/65	D	b		Tinsley
D6963	37.263	VF952	3523	2/65	D	b		Tinsley
D6964	37.264	VF953	3524	2/65	D	i		Tinsley
D6965	37.265	VF954	3525	2/65	D	i		Tinsley
D6966	37.266	VF955	3526	3/65	D	b		Tinsley
D6967	37.267	VF956	3527	3/65	D	b		Tinsley
D6968	37.268	VF957	3528	3/65	D	b		Tinsley
D6969	37.269	VF958	3529	3/65	D	o	*	Canton
D6970	37.270	VF959	3530	3/65	D	o	*	Canton
D6971	37.271	VF960	3531	4/65	D	o	*	Llandore
D6972	37.272	VF961	3532	4/65	D	o	*	Canton
D6973	37.273	VF962	3533	5/65	D	o	*	Canton
D6974	37.274	VF963	3534	5/65	D	o		Canton
D6975	37.275	VF964	3535	5/65	D	o	*	Canton
D6976	37.276	VF965	3536	5/65	D	o	*	Canton
D6977	37.277	VF966	3537	5/65	D	o	*	Canton
D6978	37.278	VF967	3538	5/65	D	o	*	Canton
D6979	37.279	VF968	3539	5/65	D	o	*	Canton
D6980	37.280	VF969	3540	6/65	D	o	*	Canton
D6981	37.281	VF970	3541	6/65	D	o	*	Canton

Original Number	TOPS Number	Works Number	EE Number	Date to Traffic	Present Status Brakes	Heat	Twin Tanks	First Allocation
D6982	37.282	VF971	3542	6/65	D	o	*	Canton
D6983	—	VF972	3543	5/65	D	o	*	Canton
D6984	37.284	VF973	3544	6/65	D	o	*	Canton
D6985	37.285	VF974	3545	6/65	D	o	*	Canton
D6986	37.286	VF975	3546	6/65	D	o	*	Canton
D6987	37.287	VF976	3547	6/65	D	o	*	Canton
D6988	37.288	VF977	3548	7/65	D	o	*	Canton
D6989	37.289	VF978	3549	7/65	D	o	*	Canton
D6990	37.290	VF979	3550	7/65	D	o	*	Canton
D6991	37.291	VF980	3551	7/65	D	o	*	Canton
D6992	37.292	VF981	3552	7/65	D	o	*	Canton
D6993	37.293	VF982	3553	7/65	D	o	*	Canton
D6994	37.294	VF983	3554	8/65	D	o	*	Canton
D6995	37.295	VF984	3555	8/65	D	o	*	Canton
D6996	37.296	VF985	3556	8/65	D	o	*	Canton
D6997	37.297	VF986	3557	8/65	D	o	*	Canton
D6998	37.298	VF987	3558	9/65	D	o	*	Canton
D6999	37.299	VF988	3559	9/65	D	o	*	Canton
D6600	37.300	VF989	3560	9/65	D	o	*	Canton
D6601	37.301	VF990	3561	9/65	D	o	*	Llandore
D6602	37.302	VF991	3562	9/65	D	o	*	Canton
D6603	37.303	VF992	3563	10/65	D	o	*	Llandore
D6604	37.304	VF993	3564	10/65	D	o	*	Llandore
D6605	37.305	VF994	3565	10/65	D	o	*	Canton
D6606	37.306	VF995	3566	10/65	D	o	*	Llandore
D6607	37.307	VF996	3567	10/65	D	o	*	Llandore
D6608	37.308	VF997	3568	1/66	D	o	*	Llandore

Key to abbreviations:

b   Locomotive fitted with operational Clayton boiler
o   Locomotive with no train heating facilities
i   Locomotive with Clayton boiler isolated

*   Twin tanks fitted
D   Dual brakes
V   Vacuum brakes

2
Specification and Control Data

Builders: English Electric Co, Vulcan Foundry; Robert Stephenson & Hawthorn Ltd
Overall length: 61ft 6in
Overall height: 12ft 10½in
Overall width: 8ft 8⅝in
Wheelbase: 50ft 8in
Bogie wheelbase: 13ft 6in
Wheel arrangement: Co-Co
Minimum radius of curve negotiable: 4 chains without gauge widening

Route availability: RA5
Wheel diameter: 3ft 7in
Gear ratio: 53 to 18
Maximum speed: 90mph
Maximum tractive effort: 55,000lb (247kN)
Continuous tractive effort: 35,000lb (156kN)
Maximum current: 2,600 amps
Fuel capacity: (i) 920gal; (ii) twin tanks, 1,720gal
Boiler fuel capacity: 120gal
Coolant capacity: 160gal

Lubricating oil capacity: 160gal
Brake equipment: Westinghouse
Maximum brake cylinder pressure: 75lb/sq in
Brake force: 50 tons
Weight (tons/cwt):
Split headcode boxes
    (i) Vacuum brake/steam heat: 104/6
    (ii) Dual brake/steam heat: 104/18
    (iii) Vacuum brake/no train heat: 102/4
    (iv) Dual brake/no train heat: 102/16
    (v) Vacuum brake/twin tanks: 105/6
    (vi) Dual brake/twin tanks: 105/18
Central headcode boxes
    (i) Vacuum brake/no heat: 104/14
    (ii) Dual brake/steam heat: 107/8
    (iii) Dual brake/no heat: 105/16
    (iv) Vacuum brake/twin tanks: 107/16
    (v) Dual brakes/twin tanks: 108/8
Diesel engine type: English Electric 12CSVT
Diesel engine horsepower: 1,750 (1,300kW) @ 850rpm;
37.292 : 2,000 (1,490kW) @ 850rpm
Diesel engine maximum rpm: 850
Diesel engine cylinders: 12 @ 10in bore × 12in stroke
Turbo chargers: 2
Main generator: EE 822/10G
    Continuous output: 1,107kW
    Continuous rating: 1,800 amps
Auxillary generator: EE911/5C
    Continuous output: 66kw
    Voltage: 110
Traction motors: (6) EE538/A
    Continuous rating: 600 amps
    One-hour rating: 630 amps
Rail hp at continuous rating: 1,250
Full power available between: 10 and 79mph
Minimum speed at continuous rating: 13.6mph
Exhausters: (2) Northey 125PE, flange-mounted
Compressors: (2) Worthington-Simpson MSV38S
Fuel transfer pump: 1
Lubricating oil pump: 1
Motor blowers: 2
Coupling restriction: Blue Star
Boiler: Clayton RO 2000
Boiler water capacity: 800gal
Battery: DP type RSKB 158 M/3 cells, 48 cells rated at
158amps/hr at 5-hour rating

Instruments and gauges in each cab
Speedometer
Vacuum gauge (Duplex)

Brake cylinder air pressure gauge
Main traction ammeter
Main reservoir air pressure gauge
Train heating steam pipe gauge
Engine stopped indicator (light) red
Fault indicator light (blue)
Wheelslip indicator light (amber)
Boiler indicator light (white)

Additional instruments and gauges in number two cab
Battery ammeter
Control air pressure gauge
Secondary indicator light system
    Oil pressure
    Fuel level
    Water   on Control Cubicle
    Blowers
Earth fault relay flag

Controls in engine room
Battery isolating switch (operated with master key)
Engine overspeed trip reset lever (on engine)
Governor over-riding hand control lever (on engine)
Radiator shutters control (handle removable)
Engine start button
Fuel priming button
Engine sump dipstick
Boiler controls
Locomotive lighting change-over switches

Controls and gauges outside locomotive
Fuel tank gauges (2)
Boiler water tank gauges (2)
Main fire extinguisher controls
Inter locomotive coupling cocks
    Main reservoir equalising pipe cocks
    Engine air control cocks
    Steam hose cocks

Fuses

	Type	Capacity
Boiler equipment	TCP	100 amp
Exhauster motor (2)	TCP	100 amp
Blower motor (2)	TFP	160 amp
Lubricating oil priming pump motor	SRW3010	30 amp
Fuel supply pump motor	SRN3007	15 amp

3
The Named Class 37s

37.012 *Loch Rannoch*
37.026 *Loch Awe*
37.027 *Loch Eil*
37.043 *Loch Lomond*
37.078 *Teesside Steelmaster*
37.081 *Loch Long*
37.180 *Sir Dyfed/County of Dyfed*
37.207 *William Cookworthy*
37.229 *The Cardiff Rod Mill*
37.260 *Radio Highland*

During spring 1963 the following locomotives were fitted with nameplates but, as a result of a change of plan, were removed by September 1963 without being unveiled to the public:

D6703 *First East Anglian Regiment*
D6704 *Second East Anglian Regiment*
D6707 *Third East Anglian Regiment*

No 37.207 *William Cookworthy* **descends the Fowey Valley on 13 December 1982 and approaches Bodmin Road with a Moorswater–Carne Point china clay train.** *John A. M. Vaughan*

Index